WALKING ON THE ORKNEY AND SHETLAND ISLES

by
Graham Uney

2 POLICE SQUARE, MILNTHORPE, CUMBRIA LA7 7PY
www.cicerone.co.uk

First edition 2009
ISBN-13: 978 1 85284 572 8

© Graham Uney 2009

A catalogue record for this book is available from the British Library.
All photographs are by the author unless otherwise stated.

OS Ordnance Survey® This product includes mapping data licenses from Ordnance Survey® with the permission of the Controller of Her Majesty's Stationery Office. © Crown copyright 2008. All rights reserved. Licence number PU100012932.

To Olivia, with love

Acknowledgements

Many thanks to the staff at Wilderness Scotland, for sending me up to Orkney and Shetland time and time again with walking and wildlife groups, and also to the editorial staff at Cicerone, for having faith in my ideas, and to Liz Inman for her painstaking and unflinching editing work.

Advice to Readers

Front cover: The Old Man of Hoy (Walk 14)

CONTENTS

SHETLAND

Mainland South

Southern Islands

Mainland Central

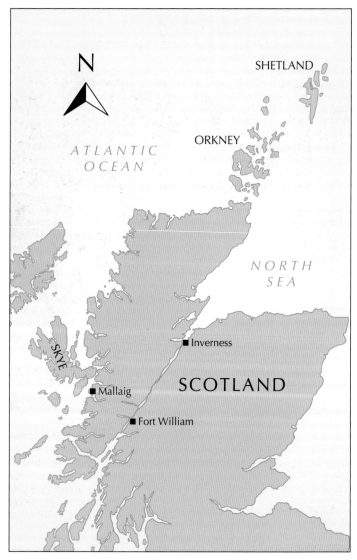

INTRODUCTION

A superb sea stack at Yesnaby (Walk 6)

Rough-edged jewels dot the wild seas to the north of mainland Britain. Here, in large group of islands known collectively as the Northern Isles of Orkney and Shetland, a vividly diverse and brazenly beautiful landscape awaits the walker. This is where those in the know come to get up close and personal with some of our most charismatic wildlife, or to discover hidden secrets from our ancient past, all set in a broad landscape of magnificent coastal crags and voes, rolling moors of heather and bilberry, small-scale farmlands of rich, flower-filled meadows,

and Scandinavian-style towns and villages thronging the steep-sided fjords of countless sea lochs. Add to this a constant big-sky feel, fresh, unpolluted air, and you have the ideal walking holiday destination.

Each island within the Northern Isles is unique. Every one is very different from its neighbours, both in terms of physical geography and character, and all have something to offer the walker. This book will lead you on the very best walks in these islands, so that you too can discover the magic of the magnificent Northern Isles.

There are walks here to suit every taste. Some are nothing more than a short stroll to an ancient site or wildlife viewpoint, whereas others are longer and require full walking gear and the knowledge of how to read a map and compass (the latter are identified as such at the start of the walk description). Few people get lost here though, as none of the islands is very big, and if it all goes a bit pear-shaped, it's usually just a simple matter of dropping down to the coast to follow it back to your starting point.

The Northern Isles themselves are made up of two distinctive groups of islands, Orkney and Shetland. These two groups are usually thought of as separate entities, and are dealt with as such in this book, although it is easily possible to link the two using ferry or air services so that you can enjoy an extended visit.

WILDLIFE

For many people visiting the Northern Isles, the superb wildlife to be found there is the main – if not the only – reason to go. This is the place to make for if you want to sit on a cliff top with puffins standing next to you just a few feet away, or if you want to watch thousands of gannets diving off a rocky headland. Perhaps you've always wanted to see an otter, or a Minke whale. Again, the place to go would be the Northern Isles.

The most obvious wildlife on the Northern Isles is the multitude of

seabirds. Both Orkney and Shetland have scores of great places to see puffins, guillemots, razorbills, black guillemots, kittiwakes, fulmars, gannets, shags and cormorants. On Orkney you should go to Marwick Head, or perhaps Deerness for the most likely sitings, while on Shetland you have even more choice, with Sumburgh Head, Esha Ness, Noss, Bressay, Hermaness, and Foula all being superb.

Shetland is also better for sightings of otters, while Orkney is the place to go for birds of prey – chiefly hen harriers, peregrines, merlins and short-eared owls.

Common and grey seals can be seen at countless locations on both Orkney and Shetland, and whales are often seen from headlands on both island groups too. Minke whales are the most likely species, although occasional orcas, pilot whales, sperm whales, and bottle-nosed whales also pass by.

In winter hundreds of thousands of ducks, geese, swans, and waders descend on Orkney and Shetland. A visit any time between late September and the end of March will give you ample opportunity to see whooper swans, barnacle geese, pink-footed geese, wigeon, teal, purple sandpipers, turnstones, sanderling and knot, all down from their Arctic breeding grounds to experience the 'balmy' Northern Isles winter!

Kittiwake at Brough Head (Walk 8)

A guillemot at St John's Head (Walk 14)

A puffin at Marwick Head (Walk 7)

ARCHAEOLOGY AND HISTORY

Another reason why Orkney and Shetland are great destinations for walking holidays is the amazing wealth of archaeological sites to be found here. While Orkney definitely has the bulk of the most impressive remains of early man, Shetland does not fall far behind.

The human history of the Northern Isles dates back to a time

before the fourth millennium BC. Places like Skara Brae, on the western shores of Orkney Mainland, and Jarlshof on South Mainland, Shetland, give clear insights into the domestic lives of the Mesolithic farming communities that settled all over this region. Their elaborate burial chambers and cairns are great fun to explore today at sites such as Culween and Wideford on Mainland

11

The Ring of Brodgar at sunset (Walk 5)

Orkney, and at Mid Howe and other sites on Rousay.

Over the years the small farming communities gradually developed into larger tribal units, which were capable of constructing major monuments such as those of Maes Howe, the Stones of Stenness and the Ring o' Brodgar.

Around 600BC the climate in the Northern Isles deteriorated. The islands became colder and wetter, and as peat and heather claimed the once-fertile high ground, upland cultivation became impossible, forcing people down to the low-lying areas. The shortage of good fertile soil meant that land became precious, and competition for farmland may have led to a more aggressive society. The construction of robust, fortified dwellings, or brochs, on both Orkney and Shetland coincided with the expansion of the bronze industry on the Scottish mainland, enabling the Orcadians to arm themselves with more sophisticated weaponry. Around 120 brochs have been recorded in Orkney alone, and there are many more on Shetland. The best preserved of these include those at Gurness and Mid Howe on Orkney, and Clickimin and Mousa on Shetland. The Mousa Broch deserves special mention as the most complete example to be found anywhere today.

The Northern Isles' first contact with Christianity was more than likely in the 6th century, but the islands can't be said to have been under church authority until the 8th century.

Norsemen began to colonise the Northern Isles in the 8th century, and before long the islands became a vital link in their western sea routes.

Exactly how the Norse takeover took place remains a hotly debated subject to this day. Whatever the circumstances, by the end of the 9th century the Norwegian settlement was firmly established.

Following the Battle of Largs in 1263, and the loss of the Western Isles as a result of the Treaty of Perth in 1266, Orkney and Shetland were the only parts of what is now Scotland to remain in Norwegian hands. But although the islands were still officially under Norse rule, the control of the Scottish earls over Orkney was increasing. The earldom was held by the Sinclairs for the Norwegian crown (and later the Danish crown) until 1468, at which time the impoverished Christian I, King of Denmark, Norway and Sweden, gave the Northern Isles to the Scottish crown as part of a marriage agreement with King James III of Scotland.

Today, the people of both Orkney and Shetland still retain close links with Scandinavia. Indeed, they do not think of themselves as Scottish, or British, at all. They are proud to be Shetlanders and Orcadians!

THE WALKS

The walking in the Northern Isles is quite varied, and the routes chosen for this book reflect this. Generally, apart from on the very shortest walks described, you'll find yourself on either open and rough moorland or hill terrain, or on coastal cliff tops.

The moorland walking on the Northern Isles lends itself to those who really want to explore. There are

An old corn drying kiln at Scatness (Walk 27)

few paths and tracks here, and you need to know how to use a map and compass effectively to follow these walks and to stay safe. Walks of this type are indicated as such at the start of the walk description.

There are no big mountains on either Orkney or Shetland, and the only big hills can be found on Hoy, to the south of Mainland Orkney, and on North Mavine, in the north of Mainland Shetland. These hills have a climate similar to that found on the Cairngorms plateau in Scotland, for despite their lowly height, the high latitudes here give them a sub-Arctic kind of terrain, and weather patterns to match.

The coastal walks tend to be relatively popular, both with walkers and birdwatchers, and many of these have the benefit of being waymarked – or at the very least have a good path running along the top of the cliffs.

In short, there really is something here for everyone, with perhaps the exception of the devoted high-peak bagger. Walkers with little or no experience will find plenty of suitable strolls, rambles and longer coastal walks to easily fill a couple of weeks, while those looking for more challenging routes and long coast traverses are also well provided for.

GETTING TO THE NORTHERN ISLES

Air
You can fly direct to either Sumburgh (Shetland) or Kirkwall (Orkney) from a number of UK airports.

The Sands of Warebeth (Walk 6)

The cliffs at Hermaness (Walk 77)

Contact British Airways and their franchise partners Logan Air on 0845 7733377 for flight information, www.loganair.co.uk.

Atlantic Airways also runs flights direct to Sumburgh from London Stanstead – tel 0845 2990777, www.flyshetland.com.

Ferry

North Link Ferries operates car ferries to Lerwick and Kirkwall from Aberdeen, or from Scrabster to Stromness (Orkney), tel 0845 6000 449, www.northlinkferries.co.uk.

Pentland Ferries operates from Gills Bay (just west of John o' Groats) to St Margaret's Hope (South Ronaldsay, Orkney), tel 01856 831226, www.pentlandferries.co.uk.

GETTING BETWEEN ORKNEY AND SHETLAND

British Airways and Logan Air run regular flights between Orkney and Shetland.

North link Ferries also runs car ferries between Lerwick and Kirkwall, on the run back to Aberdeen.

For details of tourist information centres, useful websites, where to stay on the islands, how to get around and recommended reading, see the information pages at the start of the Orkney and Shetland sections, below.

WHEN TO GO

The Northern Isles are worth a visit at any time of year, although probably the best months are April, May and

15

St John's Head (Walk 14)

June. Then you generally get the warmest, driest weather, and long days too (in Shetland they call this the 'simmer dim', and certainly around midsummer's day you can expect practically 24 hours of daylight). This is also the best time to visit if you want to see hundreds of thousands of seabirds on their nesting cliffs.

One major issue for most people when they are planning a walking holiday to anywhere in Scotland is the dreaded midge – a tiresome insect that plagues the Highlands by the million. Not so here! Orkney and Shetland are both relatively free from midges, apart from a few on the very stillest of days on Hoy (fortunately, you don't get too many very still days anywhere in the Northern Isles!).

Other times of the year can be great for a walking holiday too. I've had a couple of weeks in Shetland in January, and although you only get a few hours' daylight at this time of year, the fantastic light, late dawns, and long, early sunsets really make up for this.

The Northern Isles rarely get much snow, other than on the highest hills, so it is easily possible to enjoy a great holiday here in any season.

WHAT TO TAKE

The trick here is not to over-do it when packing. You'll definitely want some lightweight walking boots, although if you don't plan on doing any of the tougher moorland or hill routes, approach shoes (outdoor-style trainers from a specialist walking retailer) will be adequate. Waterproofs are essential, as are warm clothes, including hat and gloves.

I can't imagine anyone heading up to the Northern Isles without a camera, and binoculars can be a real asset too.

A lightweight torch can be useful for looking in brochs, tombs and other ancient monuments, but don't expect to need it for walking in summer, as it never gets dark.

For eating out, most people dress fairly casually, and when it gets cold, Norwegian-style knitwear is de rigueur! Don't worry if you don't have a 'woolly pully' or a hat – there are plenty of places to buy them throughout the islands.

If you plan on camping in the Northern Isles, you'll need all the usual – tents, sleeping bags, thermarests, stoves – and it's best to get used to using these at home first.

MAPS AND ACCESS

For all of the walks in this guide I would recommend taking along the relevant Ordnance Survey Explorer sheets. The islands are covered by 10 sheets at this scale (1:25,000), as follows:

- Orkney – OS Explorer sheets 461, 462, 463, 464, 465
- Shetland – OS Explorer sheets 466, 467, 468, 469, 470.

Also useful for general planning purposes is the Ordnance Survey Travel

Map – Northern Scotland, Orkney & Shetland – at a scale of 1:250,000.

Access in both Orkney and Shetland has always been accepted as a right, as long as you are responsible. This means leaving nothing behind (yes, even apple cores and banana skins), leaving farm gates as you find them, not entering private gardens, respecting the wildlife and the countryside in general, keeping your dog on a lead, keeping noise levels to a minimum, and being aware of and respecting all other countryside users.

HOW THIS GUIDE WORKS

Orkney is described first, beginning with a detailed introduction to that island group. The introduction tells you how to get there, how to get around, where to stay, where to get information, the general topography of the island within the group, and other useful information. The walks on Orkney then follow. Shetland is described separately, and the section on this island group also starts with the same detailed information as for Orkney.

There are 80 walks in total, some of which are short strolls, while others take you on challenging hikes along wild coastlines or to the tops of the highest hills of these wonderful islands.

All the routes within this guide are laid out in a set format. They begin with a route information box for each walk, detailing the start and finish points for the walk, and including grid references. The distance is then given in

both kilometres and miles, followed by the average time it takes to do the route. Where time should be allowed for visiting archaeological sites, for example, or for birdwatching, this is included in the average time.

These timings are all based on my experience of leading these walks with walking groups who are keen to discover their surroundings. If you simply want to go for a walk, and don't intend to spend any time visiting sites or stopping at wildlife viewpoints, then you'll definitely complete the routes faster than the suggested time.

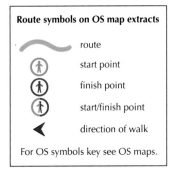

Route symbols on OS map extracts

〰️　route

🚶　start point

🚶　finish point

🚶　start/finish point

◀　direction of walk

For OS symbols key see OS maps.

Details are then given of the Ordnance Survey maps needed for each walk – I have given both Explorer (1:25,000) sheet numbers and Landranger (1:50,000) sheet numbers, as I know that many people favour either one scale or the other.

The route description then follows, with the direction to be taken, plus tips on what to look out for along the way.

ORKNEY

Walkers enjoying the coastal scenery at The Gloup (Walk 1)

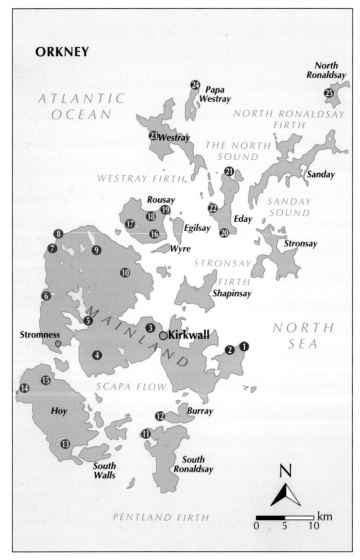

ORKNEY

North Ronaldsay

ATLANTIC OCEAN

㉔ *Papa Westray*

㉕

NORTH RONALDSAY FIRTH

㉓*Westray*

THE NORTH SOUND

WESTRAY FIRTH

㉑

Sanday

㉒

Rousay

㉓㉙ ㉘

㉗ ㉖

Egilsay

㉚

Eday

SANDAY SOUND

㉘

Wyre

Stronsay

⑧

⑦ ⑨

STRONSAY

⑩

Shapinsay

FIRTH

⑥

MAINLAND

NORTH SEA

⑤

③ ○**Kirkwall**

Stromness

④

② ①

⑮

SCAPA FLOW

⑭

Hoy

Burray

⑫

⑬

⑪

South Walls

South Ronaldsay

N

PENTLAND FIRTH

km
0   5   10

WALKING ON ORKNEY

In contrast to the islands of Shetland, Orkney has a lot more in common with other parts of Scotland. Indeed, it is not that far across the Pentland Firth to the southern islands in the Orkney group, South Ronaldsay and Hoy, from the main headlands on the northern fringes of Caithness, Dunnet Head and Duncansby Head.

Orkney's central island is called Mainland (as is that of Shetland). Mainland is odd in shape – a glance at a map reveals that the western end is roughly circular, and is connected to the eastern side by a narrow neck upon which Kirkwall, the island's capital has been built. To the south of Mainland some important islands form a ring around the huge and strategic seaway of Scapa Flow. These southern islands include Hoy, Graemsay, Flotta, Burray and South Ronaldsay, while to the north the islands are much further flung, and include Shapinsay, Stronsay, Sanday, North Ronaldsay, Eday, Papa Westray, Westray and Rousay.

Orkney has a very different feel to Shetland. Much of the land here is gently rolling, and often farmed. There is a lot of arable land on Orkney, and lots of wildflower meadows let over to pasture for cows and sheep.

Not all of Orkney is agricultural. Large parts of the centre of Mainland offer moorland walking, while the islands of Hoy and Rousay are quite hilly, offering wild and remote walks for those with a will to explore.

For many people, though, the whole focus of a holiday on Orkney is the rich archaeological heritage to be found there. Surely Orkney has more important sites per square mile of land than anywhere else in the world (and in that statement I include Egypt!)

The wildlife here is fantastic too. Although there are not the huge seabird colonies found in Shetland, Orkney has good numbers of raptors, such as hen harriers, and short-eared owls, both of which are not usually found on Shetland.

Getting There

Fly to Kirkwall, the main airport on Orkney, from Edinburgh, Glasgow, Aberdeen and Inverness. Contact British Airways and their franchise partners Logan Air on 0845 7733377 for flight information, www.loganair.co.uk.

North Link Ferries runs car ferries to Kirkwall from Aberdeen, or Stromness from Scrabster, tel 0845 6000 449, www.northlinkferries.co.uk.

Pentland Ferries operates from Gills Bay (just west of John o' Groats) to St Margaret's Hope (South Ronaldsay), tel 01856 831226, www.pentlandferries.co.uk.

Getting Around

For car hire contact Orkney Car Hire in Kirkwall, tel 01856 872866, www.orkneycarhire.co.uk.

For local buses, contact Orkney public transport on 01856 873535, www.orkneypublictransport.co.uk.

For ferries to the islands, contact Orkney Ferries, tel 0800 0113648, www.orkneyferries.co.uk.

Where to Stay

I usually stay at Woodwick House near Evie, tel 01856 751330, www.woodwickhouse.co.uk.

For other ideas for accommodation, including hotels, guesthouses, bed and breakfast, hostels, self-catering and campsites, the Orkney Tourist Board is superb, tel 01856 872856, www.visitorkney.com.

Tourist Information Offices

The Travel Centre, West Castle Street, Kirkwall, Orkney, tel 01856 872856, www.visitorkney.com.

Stromness Travel Centre, Pier Head, Stromness, Orkney, tel 01856 850716.

Useful Books

The Orkney Guidebook by Charles Tait.

A Souvenir Guide to Orkney by Charles Tait.

Orkney, a Historical Guide by Caroline Wickham-Jones.

Sillocks, Skarfies and Selkies – the Fish, Amphibians, Reptiles, Birds and Mammals of Orkney by Chris and Jean Booth.

Isles of the North by Ian Mitchell.

The Islands of Scotland by Hamish Haswell Smith.

Backpacker's Britain Vol 3: Northern Scotland by Graham Uney.

Skara Brae (Walk 6)

ORKNEY MAINLAND

WALK 1

Mull Head and the Brough of Deerness

Start/finish	Park at the car park by the Gloup. There is a visitor centre with toilets here too.
Grid ref	HY589079
Distance	7.2km/4.5 miles
Time	3–4 hours
Maps	OS Explorer 461; OS Landranger 6

It's a good idea to have a look round the visitor centre before you start the walk. It lies just north of the car park, on the opposite side of the road. The visitor centre has some fascinating displays on the geology, wildlife and social history of the Deerness peninsula.

A lovely walk around this popular headland. The walk takes in the Mull Head Nature Reserve, which holds important numbers of seabirds.

From the car park head east along a waymarked path. Within 200m you'll come to a viewing platform on the right, which gives an impressive glimpse into the great gulf known as the Gloup.

The Gloup is an extended blow-hole, formed as the waves have found a weakness in the geology of the cliffs. A way has been forced through by the power of the sea, and over thousands of years the gulf has grown longer and wider. It is a spectacular sight, particularly in stormy weather. The walls of the Gloup are a good place to see black guillemots, or tysties, as the locals call them.

Continue to the arch forming the Gloup, where you'll find another viewing platform, then pass through a gate and head north along the broken rocks of Clu Ber, the cliff tops leading towards the Brough of Deerness. Keep close to the cliff edge for great views of shags, kittiwakes,

23

and fulmars, while seals can often be seen hauled out on the rocks at the base of the cliffs.

You soon come to the rocky headland of Brough of Deerness. This is almost an island, and has a very narrow neck connecting it to the rest of Deerness. To reach the top of the brough you descend a flight of wooden steps into the bay on the north side. Now squeeze through a rocky cleft and pick up a path leading to the top. The path is narrow and shaly, and has a drop down the right-hand side into a rocky cove, but the way is easy, and there is a fixed chain for you to hang onto. ◀

The Brough of Deerness shows signs of an ancient settlement. There are earthworks visible around the remains of a chapel.

Return to the main cliff top via the narrow cleft and flight of wooden steps. Now continue northwards, following the coast closely to get the best views into the hidden coves and geos. Soon after the brough you pass through a gate and out onto the moorland of Mull Head. Great skuas, Arctic skuas, golden plover, curlew and dunlin all nest on these moors.

Continue around the headland, deviating slightly to climb to the Ordnance Survey trig point on the left. This marks the high point of Mull Head, at 48m, although the land further in towards the Ward of Deerness is much higher.

Beyond Mull Head the coast turns to the southwest, and you follow the path around the broad bay of Den Wick. A mile from Mull Head you come to a path junction beside a signpost. Straight ahead lies the Deerness Memorial (see the next walk), while the return to your car lies to the left.

Follow a path through heather with the fence to your right, and you soon come to a track cutting across at right angles. Turn right here and walk towards the farm at Denwick, on a track between

Enjoying the views from Mull Head

fences. The route is obvious and is marked by posts throughout.

At Denwick turn left onto a good track heading southeast and follow this to where it splits, with a track running along both sides of a fence. It doesn't really matter which of these parallel tracks you take, although the official route is the one to the right of the fence.

Where the track to the left of the fence swings away to the left, continue straight ahead over a little hill and you soon reach the farm at Breckan, beside an electric fence on the right.

At the cairn below Mull Head

25

Stay on the path to the end of the farm enclosure, then turn left to follow it down to the road just right of the car park.

WALK 2
The Deerness Memorial

Start/finish	Park at end of the B9051, near Northqouy Point.
Grid ref	HY554074
Distance	7.2km/4.5 miles
Time	3–4 hours
Maps	OS Explorer 461; OS Landranger 6

A pleasant walk to the Deerness Memorial.

From Northqouy Point walk northeastwards along the coast, passing low cliffs where fulmars nest on your left. There is a path along the cliff top that takes you beside wildflower meadows until you reach the memorial.

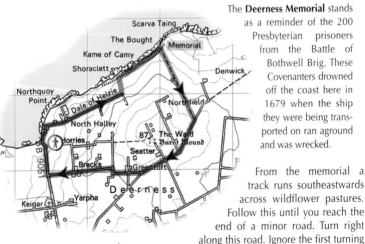

The **Deerness Memorial** stands as a reminder of the 200 Presbyterian prisoners from the Battle of Bothwell Brig. These Covenanters drowned off the coast here in 1679 when the ship they were being transported on ran aground and was wrecked.

From the memorial a track runs southeastwards across wildflower pastures. Follow this until you reach the end of a minor road. Turn right along this road. Ignore the first turning to the right, and walk on to a crossroads.

Go straight ahead here, then veer right at a Y-junction.

At Greentoft continue straight ahead again until you come to a T-junction. Now turn right, then left immediately. The lane now takes you on through the Brecks to a T-junction where you meet the B9051. Turn right to return to your car.

WALK 3
Wideford Hill

Start/finish	Park at the small car park on the side of Wideford Hill, at the bend in the minor road above Heathfield Farm.
Grid ref	HY410114
Distance	5.1km/3.2 miles
Time	2–3 hours
Maps	OS Explorer 463; OS Landranger 6

From the car park, start by heading steeply uphill towards the summit at 225m. The route is via the lane that ends on the top, among a cluster of masts and attendant buildings. Have a wander around the summit area, taking in the magnificent views.

The views down the east side of **Wideford Hill** to Kirkwall are superb, but add to this the extensive panorama you get on all sides and you have a truly memorable experience. To the north most of the islands can be seen, including Shapinsay, Rousay, Stronsay, Eday, Sanday and North Ronaldsay. The views to the south stretch over Scapa Flow to distant Scotland, while the hills of Hoy fill the view to the southwest.

Now head west, down the steep slopes, until you hit a path that cuts diagonally downhill. Turn right and follow this path down to a path junction. Continue in the same direction, just west of north, until you reach the wonderful remains of the Wideford Chambered Cairn.

A fine walk to the summit of Wideford Hill, giving superb views over Kirkwall and the islands scattered around Mainland, and taking in the important chambered cairn on the slopes of Wideford Hill.

The **cairn** is great fun to visit. You drop into the burial chamber via a hatch and then find three cells and a long entrance passage. An excavation here in 1935 revealed the internal structure of the cairn, and parts of this were left exposed so that today you can see the revetment walls that held the cairn in place.

Return along the path, climbing diagonally to the junction that you passed earlier. You can continue on the path to the left to retrace your route directly back to your car, or you can drop down to the right, contouring for a little way before you descend to the minor road at Haughhead. Here turn left, following the lane to the junction below Heathfield Farm. Turn left uphill and follow the lane back to your car.

Ruin on Wideford Hill

WALK 4
Ward Hill

Start/finish	Park at the top of the hill above Scorra Dale – there are lay-bys on either side of the road here.
Grid ref	HY322054
Distance	9.6km/6 miles
Time	3–4 hours
Map	OS Explorer 463; OS Landranger 6
Note	Map and compass skills required.

From the parking area at the top of the minor road there is a track leading northwards. Follow this around the west side of Hill of Dale, then, when it becomes a little narrower, follow the path up the steep slopes onto Gruf Hill. The path leads just west of north, then swings to the right as the summit ridge is gained. The top is marked by a small cairn at 189m.

The path continues over the summit to the northeast, dropping steadily down the other side to a junction of

A wild moorland route leading to the highest hill on Mainland.

The views from the summit of Ward Hill, particularly to the southwest towards Hoy, are very impressive.

tracks on the col between Gruf Hill and Ward Hill. The slopes up to the top of Ward Hill form a fairly obvious ridge, and lead quite steeply up to the Ordnance Survey triangulation pillar at 268m. ◀

Return down the southwest ridge to the col, then, where the tracks all meet, turn left and follow the track down into Rams Dale. At first the track heads straight down the valley, but soon veers away to the right and clings to the west side instead.

Stay on the track all the way down to the main A964 in Orphir. Turn right and follow the road to the big bend at Scorra Dale. Take the narrow lane on the right here, climbing up to the top of the hill where you parked your car.

WALK 5

The Ring of Brodgar and the Stones of Stenness

Start/finish	Park at the large new car park (not yet marked on the OS maps) on the east side of the B9055, just north of the Ring of Brodgar.
Grid ref	HY294136
Distance	10km/6.2 miles
Time	3–4 hours
Maps	OS Explorer 463; OS Landranger 6
Note	To visit the tomb of Maes Howe you have to book a time for a guided tour. Telephone the visitor centre on 01856 761606 to do this.

An easy walk along a road to visit three of the most remarkable and archaeologically important sites in Britain.

From the car park cross the road and follow the signed path to the Ring of Brodgar Stone Circle.

The **Ring of Brodgar** is the largest stone circle in Scotland. It is more than 100m across, and originally had 60 stones all set in a perfect circle. It dates from around 3000BC, making it contemporary with the Great Pyramids of Egypt. One of the greatest things about the Ring of Brodgar is its setting. This stone circle

The Ring of Brodgar ancient stone circle

lies between Loch of Harray and Loch of Stenness, and from a nearby chambered cairn the views out to Hoy across Loch of Stenness are magnificent.

Once you've pottered around the Ring of Brodgar, head southeast across the grassy meadow, aiming for a single standing stone, known as the Comet Stone. From here you pass through a gate

and out onto the B9055. Turn right along the road, going over a causeway on your way towards the Stones of Stenness.

Before you get to the Stones of Stenness, however, there is a path on the left that leads beside the field in which the stones stand. Take this path down to the Barnhouse Village.

The **Barnhouse Village** also dates back to 3000BC. When it was excavated it was decided to reconstruct the original site alongside, then to cover over the old buildings to preserve them. However, it is worth visiting the site to get a feel for how Neolithic man was living in these areas, and it is only a short detour.

The Standing Stones of Stenness are huge. The layout at this 5000-year-old site is simple, but it is this simplicity that is one of its chief attractions.

Return along the path towards the road, but climb a stile on the left to take you into the field where the Standing Stones of Stenness can be found. ◄

The Stones of Stenness

Walk out onto the B9055 and turn left again, continuing to the junction with the A965. Away over to your left is a large grassy mound. This is Maes Howe, your next destination.

Walk along the road to the visitor centre at Tormiston Mill, on the right. You will need to book a timed tour to visit Maes Howe, and Tormiston Mill is the starting point for the visit.

Maes Howe is considered by many to be the finest monument in the whole of Britain. It is certainly impressive. Although the mound of grass doesn't look much from the outside, what it hides is a 5000-year-old tomb. The structure is amazing, partly because of its intricate and carefully planned design, but also because of the huge size of the blocks of rock used in its building. As you enter, take a look at the huge single stone that forms the left-hand side of the entrance passage. The guide on your tour will tell you all about the other interesting features of the tomb, including how the Vikings broke in through the roof in the 11th century, adding graffiti to the walls in the form of runes.

Once your tour at Maes Howe is finished, make your way back along the road to the Ring of Brodgar, returning via the same route as your outward one.

WALK 6

Skara Brae, Yesnaby and Stromness

Start	The Bay of Skaill car park
Grid ref	HY236193
Finish	Stromness
Grid ref	HY253087
Distance	26.2km/16.3 miles
Time	8–10 hours
Maps	OS Explorer 463; OS Landranger 6
Note	This walk is linear – to return to your car, a taxi from Stromness harbour back to the Bay of Skaill will cost about £10.

This long and remote walk starts at the Bay of Skaill, where you'll find Skaill House and the entrance to Skara Brae.

Drop down onto the beach and walk around the outside of the Skara Brae complex until you can regain the cliff top. Continue around the headland to Hole o' Row, a fine natural arch. The route continues around Yettna Geo to Row Head then on to the Broch o' Borwick.

Walkers at Skara Brae

SKAILL HOUSE AND SKARA BRAE

Skaill House is an early-17th-century mansion containing a few interesting artefacts, including the dinner service from Captain Cook's Resolution, but all this is not terribly exciting when Skara Brae lies just a few hundred metres down the track!

Skara Brae rose from the sand dunes in a violent storm during 1850. The sand was blown off the remains of this 5000-year-old site, revealing to the world the best-preserved Stone Age village in northern Europe. It is known that the site was occupied for around 600 years from about 3000BC, and you can still see the stone furniture, fireplaces, drains, and even damp-proof coursing in the foundations! The entrance to Skara Brae is through a modern visitor centre, and there is a charge.

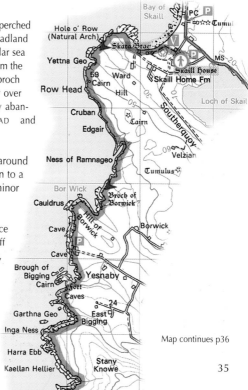

The **Broch o' Borwick** is perched high on an eroding headland surrounded by spectacular sea cliffs. Thought to date from the first millennium BC, the broch was probably in use for over 1000 years, until finally abandoned between 500AD and 600AD.

From here you head around the Hill of Borwick and on to a car park at the end of a minor road at Yesnaby.

Yesnaby is a lovely place for a walk. The cliff scenery here is amazing, and it also happens to be one of the best places in the Northern Isles to find that rare plant the Scottish Primrose, *Primula scotica*.

Map continues p36

35

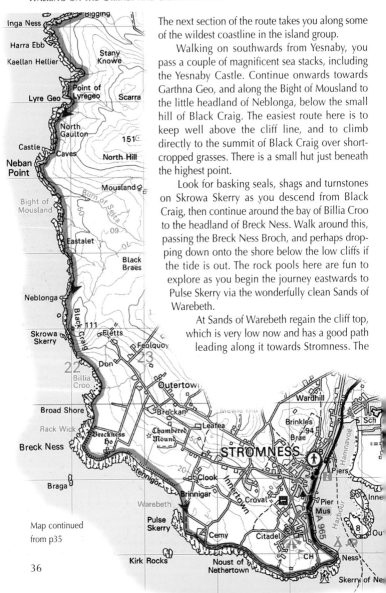

The next section of the route takes you along some of the wildest coastline in the island group.

Walking on southwards from Yesnaby, you pass a couple of magnificent sea stacks, including the Yesnaby Castle. Continue onwards towards Garthna Geo, and along the Bight of Mousland to the little headland of Neblonga, below the small hill of Black Craig. The easiest route here is to keep well above the cliff line, and to climb directly to the summit of Black Craig over short-cropped grasses. There is a small hut just beneath the highest point.

Look for basking seals, shags and turnstones on Skrowa Skerry as you descend from Black Craig, then continue around the bay of Billia Croo to the headland of Breck Ness. Walk around this, passing the Breck Ness Broch, and perhaps dropping down onto the shore below the low cliffs if the tide is out. The rock pools here are fun to explore as you begin the journey eastwards to Pulse Skerry via the wonderfully clean Sands of Warebeth.

At Sands of Warebeth regain the cliff top, which is very low now and has a good path leading along it towards Stromness. The

Map continued from p35

36

The coast at Yesnaby

Stromness harbour

walking here is easy, but pleasant, and you soon find yourself on a minor road leading around a golf course and into the centre of Stromness.

Stromness is the second biggest town on Orkney, after Kirkwall. It sits on the natural harbour of Hamnavoe. In the 18th century the growth in the whaling industry made it an important last port of call for ships heading north to the cold waters of Greenland. Many local men were recruited into the ranks of crewmen on these whaling ships.

As you walk around Skerry of Ness, the last headland before you turn the corner into the town proper, look for seals on the rocks here at low tide.

WALK 7
Marwick Head and the Kitchener Memorial

Start/finish	The small car park overlooking Mar Wick.
Grid ref	HY230242
Distance	9.6km/6 miles
Time	3–4 hours
Maps	OS Explorer 463; OS Landranger 6

Start by walking northwards to the far end of the car park. There's a gateway with a signpost for Marwick Head here, and a path takes you behind a shingle bank. Follow this path, listening for calling corncrakes during the summer months.

At the far end of the shingle bank you emerge on a grassy path that leads westwards above the bay, and around to the cliff tops at Choldertoo. Have a look over the edge in one or two places as you go, as there are countless ledges for puffins, guillemots and razorbills to nest on.

As you round the headland at Choldertoo there is a first view of the huge tower of the Kitchener Memorial.

The RSPB reserve at Marwick Head gives a superb cliff-top walk full of great views all round, and seabirds in their thousands packed onto the cliffs.

The **Kitchener Memorial** was erected in 1926, after the First World War, to commemorate Lord Kitchener and the crew of the HMS Hampshire, which was sunk off this coast in 1916 by a German mine. Only 12 of her crew survived. Kitchener was then Minster of War, and in June that year he had arrived in

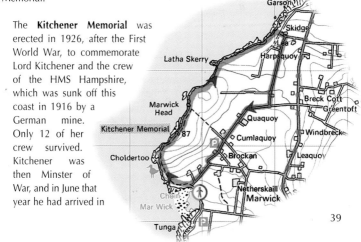

Scapa Flow to visit Admiral Jellicoe to discuss his account of the Battle of Jutland.

Continue walking northeastwards, keeping a watchful eye on the amazing spectacle of thousands of birds all crammed onto ledges in this seabird city. Beyond the Kitchener Memorial the cliffs drop in height as you reach Latha Skerry. Walk on until you come to the farm at Harpsquoy, and here bear right onto a track.

The track leads eastwards onto another track in a short distance, and here you turn southwards, following the lovely green lane as lapwings whirl above, skylarks fill the air with their song, and rabbits dash for cover.

The green lane comes out onto a metalled road, where you turn right, following the road around the bend to Quaquoy and onwards to Brockan. Go straight ahead at the point where a track crosses over the road, and continue downhill to a sharp bend to the left. Immediately after this bend you reach another metalled lane, and here you turn right, down to the coast.

Marwick Head RSPB reserve and the Kitchener Memorial

This is the point at the north end of the shingle bank you passed earlier. Turn left and go through a little gate, leading behind the shingle bank. Retrace your steps to the car park.

Walkers descending from Marwick Head

WALK 8
Brough Head

Start/finish	The Brough of Birsay car park
Grid ref	HY243283
Distance	2.6km/1.6 miles
Time	1–2 hours
Maps	OS Explorer 463; OS Landranger 6
Note	The short spit of land that connects the Brough of Birsay to Mainland is only accessible at low tides, so be careful not to get stranded. Telephone the Earl's Palace to check tide times, 01856 721205.

The Brough of Birsay

This walk around a cliff-top path offers good views of nesting birds in early summer. There is a small charge for visiting the island, payable to Historic Scotland at the kiosk.

The small island of the **Brough of Birsay** lies at the northwestern tip of Mainland Orkney. It was an important Pictish stronghold from around the sixth century, and many interesting archaeological remains have been found here from this period.

Once you are on the island there is no need for a detailed description of the walk, as it is very simple to follow the coast. The route takes you anticlockwise around the cliff-top path, where you should see puffins, guillemots, razorbills and fulmars nesting during the early summer. If you don't want to go right round the island, there is a path from

the lighthouse, on the very western tip of the island, that goes back to the spit.

Walkers enjoying the Brough of Birsay

Once you've enjoyed the walk, return to the kiosk on Mainland via the scramble across wrack- and weed-covered rocks.

WALK 9

The Loch of Hundland and Mid Hill

Start/finish	Park sensibly on the roadside along the minor road running northwest to Kirbuster from the B9057.
Grid ref	HY318238
Distance	22.5km/14 miles
Time	6–7 hours
Maps	OS Explorer 463; OS Landranger 6
Note	Map and compass skills required.

A long walk taking in the whole of the Loch of Hundland, plus a climb up onto the Birsay Moors to Mid Hill.

From the roadside just west of Skelday a track heads northwards up the rough ground towards Skelday Hill. Follow this until you are clear of the meadows in the dale, and out on the open moor. The track continues to the northeast, climbing gently all the while, leading you up to the summit of Mid Hill at 193m. The top is marked by an OS trig point.

The **Birsay Moors** are managed as an RSPB nature reserve, primarily as a great nesting site for birds of prey. You might be lucky enough to spot hunting hen harriers in this area, or perhaps a dashing merlin. The area is also a good place to see short-eared owls hunting. Other birds that nest on the moors include golden plovers, dunlin, curlews, whimbrel and Arctic skuas.

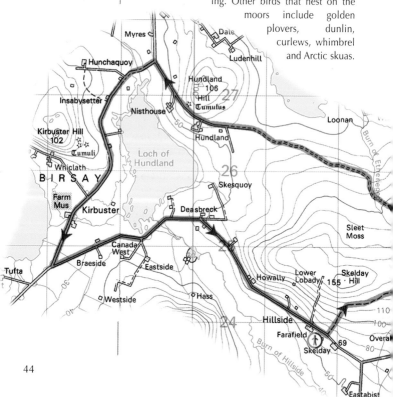

Mid Hill from Woodwick House

From the summit of Mid Hill there are tracks running off in a northwesterly direction. Follow these downhill to the Burn of Etheriegeo, and cross over the stream to the other side. The track continues to the northwest, giving you superb views across the Loch of Swannay to the north.

Eventually the track drops down to the farm at Hundland, and you should continue walking northwestwards out onto a minor road. This leads you around the north side of the Loch of Hundland, and although you are a good way from its banks, you can still get great views across the shining flats.

At a T-junction in the road, turn left and follow the lane southwards, ignoring the turn to the right at Kirbuster. Continue along the lane, passing a farm museum, then take the next left, turning back sharply on itself.

This lane takes you around the south shores of the Loch of Hundland, curving around eventually to the southeast and passing above the wild mires of Hillside to the right. Continue along the quiet lane until you reach your car parked near Skelday.

45

WALK 10

Fibla Field and Mid Tooin

Start/finish	Park sensibly on the roadside along the minor road near Graemshall, just off the A966 near Tingwall.
Grid ref	HY393222
Distance	11.4km/7.1 miles
Time	3–4 hours
Maps	OS Explorer 463; OS Landranger 6
Note	Map and compass skills required.

A pleasant walk to the prominent hill overlooking the north side of Mainland and the island of Rousay.

From the minor road at Graemshall set off on foot along the lane. You should pass a turn off to the right, then another to the left, ignoring both. Soon the lane becomes a track, and takes you in a general westerly direction up around the southern flanks of Hammars Hill.

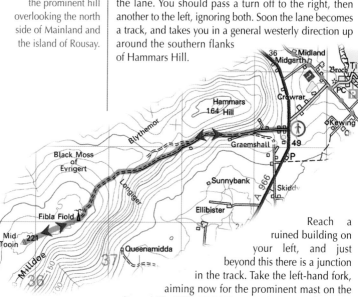

Reach a ruined building on your left, and just beyond this there is a junction in the track. Take the left-hand fork, aiming now for the prominent mast on the distant hill of Fibla Field. The going is easy, as the gradient is never too steep, and the track gives good footing.

At Fibla Field you come to the obvious mast, while ahead to the southwest, across half a mile of rough

moorland, you can make out the summit of Mid Tooin, marked by an Ordnance Survey trig point. Aim for the trig point, and cross the moorland to reach the summit at 221m.

The views to the north over Rousay are stunning. Rousay is revealed as being surprisingly hilly, and will whet your appetite for the wonderful walking to be found over there.

Turn to the northeast and retrace your steps to your car.

Mid Tooin from Click Mill

Click Mill

SOUTHERN ISLANDS

WALK 11

South Ronaldsay – Hoxa Head

Start/finish	There is a small car park at Uppertown, just west of Hoxa.
Grid ref	ND408933
Distance	1.9km/1.2 miles
Time	1 hour
Maps	OS Explorer 461; OS Landranger 7

A short walk overlooking the huge expanse of Scapa Flow.

From the car park walk on to the southwest, along the lane to the Bu. Here you'll see a footpath cutting down to the right, towards the northwest coast of the headland. Follow this path down to the low cliff top, and then turn left.

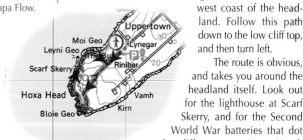

The route is obvious, and takes you around the headland itself. Look out for the lighthouse at Scarf Skerry, and for the Second World War batteries that dot the cliff tops near Hoxa Head.

SCAPA FLOW

Scapa Flow is a huge natural harbour. It has been used as such for hundreds of years, from the time of the Viking warships of King Haakon to the present day, and proved essential to the British fleet during both world wars.

During the First World War a German U-boat was seen in Scapa Flow, and merchant ships were put in place across many of the entrances as block-ships to stop further enemy intrusion into this strategic base. ▶

◀ After the armistice, 74 ships of the German High Seas Fleet were interned in Scapa Flow. They arrived in November 1918, and during the 10 months they were there the ships became something of a tourist attraction. When Rear Admiral von Reuter, the German officer in command of the fleet in Scapa Flow, realised that Germany would have to accept terms of surrender, he ordered all of the ships under his command to be scuttled. Many were sunk, and some were beached. The beached ships were quickly removed, but it took until the 1920s to get the huge salvage operation underway for the sunken ships. There are now just eight scuttled ships remaining in Scapa Flow.

Walk on around Hoxa Head, continuing to the southern tip at Bloie Geo. From here a track takes you northwards, slightly inland. Pass a track going off to the right, then almost immediately you'll come to another. Take this, walking in a northeasterly direction until you hit the road end at the Bu. Your car is parked just along the road.

WALK 12
Burray – the Hunda Reef

Start/finish	Ask if you can park at the craft shop at Littlequoy.
Grid ref	ND450965
Distance	5.4km/3.4 miles
Time	1–2 hours
Maps	OS Explorer 461; OS Landranger 6 or 7

From the farm at Littleqouy, now a craft centre, follow a track through the buildings and down to the shore. The track becomes a path as it passes over the stony shelf that is the Hunda Reef.

The island if Hunda is small, and needs little in way of description. This walk goes around the coast in an anticlockwise direction, although you are free to wander at will.

Off the west side of Burray is Hunda, a small islet connected to Burray by a stony reef. A walk around Hunda's shores is a pleasant way to spend a couple of hours.

Scapa Flow and Hunda

BURRAY CAUSEWAYS

Burray is connected to Mainland to the north via causeways that cut across to the small islands of Glimps Holm and Lamb Holm. To the south, another causeway connects Burray to South Ronaldsay.

These causeways were built during the Second World War. The British Home Fleet was based in Scapa Flow, from where it helped to protect the Arctic convoys to Murmansk. On the night of 13 October, only a month after war had been declared, the German U-boat U-47 slipped between Mainland and Lamb Holm, squeezing by the sunken block-ships that had been placed there during the First World War. Just after midnight the U-Boat commander, Lieutenant Gunther Prien, sighted the HMS Royal Oak. He ordered torpedoes to be fired at the huge ship, and a hole 9m (30 feet) in diameter was made in the hull, sinking the Royal Oak. Of the crew of 1400 men, 833 lost their lives that night.

Following this event, further block-ships were put in place, until 1940, when Churchill gave orders to have permanent concrete blocks put across the gaps between the islands. The causeways that we drive over today are built on these same Churchill Barriers. On many of them you can still see the original block-ships on either side.

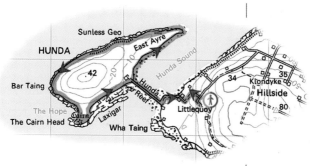

From East Ayre, the peninsula at the
northern end of the island, you get a good view across
to Churchill Barrier No 3, which blocked access to
Scapa Flow between the islands of Burray and Glimps
Holm. You can also see the next small island to the
north, Lamb Holm, where Italian prisoners of war were
kept during the Second World War. On the island they
built a remarkable chapel, using two Nissen huts and
any bits of scrap that they could find or beg. The
chapel is still there today, and is well worth a visit.

Enjoy the views from the island of Hunda out across
the vast expanse of Scapa Flow, then return to the Hunda
Reef and cross back over to Littlequoy.

WALK 13
Hoy – Heldale Water and Tor Ness

Start/finish	Park at Heldale, on the side of the B9047, overlooking North Bay on the island of Hoy.
Grid ref	ND284913
Distance	17.7km/11 miles
Time	6–7 hours
Maps	OS Explorer 462; OS Landranger 7
Note	Map and compass skills required.

A rough and wild walk into one of the more remote parts of the island of Hoy.

Start by following the good track northwestwards across the moor from Heldale. The going is easy, and the gradient slight. Keep to the north side of the Burn of Heldale, and soon reach a building beside a junction. Ignore the track cutting up the hillside to the right, towards Binga Fea, but instead go straight ahead, dropping slightly to cross the burn.

The track continues to the eastern end of Heldale Water. Your route takes you further westwards to the coast, and to get there you must walk alongside Heldale Water. I usually go along the south side of the loch, beneath the steep ground of Skird Hill, but it is slightly easier, though longer, to walk along the north bank.

Either way, you'll end up at the western end of Heldale Water. Now cut across the open moor to the southwest, aiming for the rocky cliffs at Sweinn Geo. Cross a stream just before you reach the cliff tops, then turn southwards along the coast.

The walking here is marvellous, and takes you into parts of the island little visited by other walkers. Continue beyond the Needle, a huge spire of rock set in a narrow gulf at the base of the cliffs, then on southwards towards the bay at Ha Wick.

As you approach Ha Wick the ground drops away, and the cliffs on your right become much lower. You get a view of the lighthouse on Tor Ness dead ahead, and a short walk will bring you up to its base.

The headland itself is a wonderful spot, and just around it to the east big dunes have built up behind Sheep Skerry.

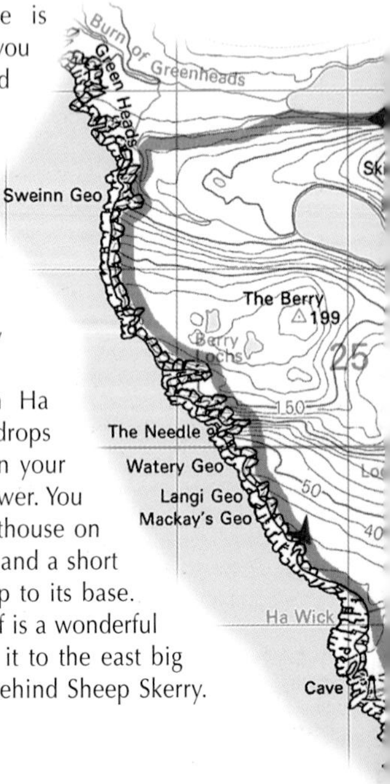

Map labels: Burn of Greenheads · Green Heads · Sweinn Geo · Ski... · The Berry △199 · Berry Lochs · 25 · 1.50 · The Needle · Watery Geo · Langi Geo · Mackay's Geo · 50 · 40 · Ha Wick · Cave

Walk eastwards across these dunes and you'll pick up a track. Follow this northeastwards, turning left at the first junction to take you to Melsetter.

Now walk out along the driveway to the farm, to gain the B9047 overlooking a huge beach on North Bay. Turn left along the road and follow it around North Bay back to your car at Heldale.

ale Water

80

Burn of Heldale

Cairn Hill
·164

150

Heldale

120

Summery

MS

26

27

28

B9047

the Berry

Saltness

Salt Ness

Melsetter
Hill
101

Melsetter

MS

Hill
Head

20

Dunes

10

tlee
oor

Sheep
Skerry

Sands Geo

Melberry

WALK 14

Hoy – The Old Man of Hoy, St John's Head and Cuilags from Rackwick

Start/finish	Park at Rackwick, down near the shore at the public toilets, on the northwestern side of Hoy.
Grid ref	ND202993
Distance	18.1km/11.3 miles
Time	7–8 hours
Maps	OS Explorer 462; OS Landranger 7
Note	Map and compass skills required.
Note	The ferry from Stromness (Mainland) to Moaness (Hoy) is passenger only. If you want to bring a car over you have to come via the Houton–Lyness route. However, for Rackwick, if you want to use the Stromness–Moaness route, you can book a taxi from Moaness (tel 01856 791315).

The Old Man of Hoy is one of the most recognisable features in the Northern Isles. The walk out to it from Rackwick is splendid, and this route continues to magnificent St John's Head.

From the car park head southwest along a track to Moss. Here, on the right, you'll see a path cutting uphill to the scattered, grass-topped houses at Moorfea. This path leads you to the youth hostel and museum, but before you reach these building you'll see a sign pointing to the southwest, to the Old Man.

Follow this path, climbing steeply at first, and then contouring as it comes closer to the edge of the cliffs. The route passes along the southern flank of the hill of Moor Fea, and gives a superb viewpoint along the wild west coast of Hoy.

As the path curves around to the northwest, it leaves the cliffs and takes you into an elevated valley, above the Loch of Stourdale. In the distance now you can see the top of the Old Man of Hoy, and a short walk along a bouldery path takes you out onto a rocky headland overlooking the huge pinnacle of sandstone.

From the cliffs overlooking the Old Man there is a path going northeast. Take this, keeping close to the cliffs and climbing steeply as you approach St John's Head.

THE OLD MAN OF HOY

The only reason the soft sandstone of the Old Man of Hoy didn't crumble away years ago is that it is standing on a bed of hard basalt. It rises 140m (450 feet) above the sea, and is fairly popular with climbers.

The stack was first climbed in 1966, over a period of three days, by Tom Patey, Rusty Baillie and Chris Bonington. The following year it featured in the first live BBC outside broadcast, when it was climbed again, this time by Bonington and Patey repeating their original route, while two new routes were put up on the same day by the teams of Pete Crew and Dougal Haston, and Ian McNaught-Davis and Joe Brown.

On 16 May 2008 the first person to base-jump off the stack was announced by BBC Radio Orkney.

The route passes massive cliffs (among the highest in Britain) before you veer off to the east to gain the highest point of the hill, at 378m. The summit of St John's Head is marked by a cairn and an OS trig point, which is set about half a mile east from the cliff edge.

The Old Man of Hoy

From the summit
follow the broad ridge to the northeast, passing a pool
and continuing along to a col between the broad corrie
of Back Saddles to the south and the rocky cliffs of
Energars to the north.

St John's Head

From the col turn to the southeast, climbing again to the wonderful cone of Cuilags. The summit is again marked by a cairn, and is at 433m.

The route off Cuilags is down the long south ridge. It is pathless for the most part, but mainly heather and grass, so the going is not too difficult. As you descend you may wish to bear off to the left slightly, as there is a path running through the glen that is easy to gain.

Once on the path turn to the southwest and follow it through the Glens of Kinnaird, passing the remnants of the ancient Hoy woodlands of Berriedale. The track

57

The Glen of Kinnaird from Rackwick, Hoy

crosses a stream via a bridge lower down, then brings you out onto the road leading into Rackwick. Turn right along the road, then go left at the junction to return to your car.

WALK 15

Hoy – Ward Hill from Moaness

Start/finish	The ferry terminal at Moaness (ferry comes in from Stromness on Mainland).
Grid ref	HY245039
Distance	15.7km/9.8 miles
Time	5–6 hours
Maps	OS Explorer 462; OS Landranger 6 or 7
Note	Map and compass skills required.
Note	The ferry from Stromness (Mainland) to Moaness (Hoy) is passenger only.

From the pier at Moaness follow the lane out to a junction with the B9047. Ignore all turns to right and left and simply stay on the dead ahead, going just south of west towards the big glen between Ward Hill and Cuilags.

Follow this lane as it climbs quite steeply uphill. Near the top of the hill, just before you reach Sandy Loch, the road turns sharply to the right. Ignore this and take the track going straight ahead. The track crosses a little stream on the right, just beneath the dam of Sandy Loch, then turns left to run along the northwestern side of the loch itself.

Beyond the loch the route climbs very slightly to a col, then begins to take you down into the Glens of Kinnaird overlooking Rackwick. As you go over the col you will notice an obvious heathery ridge coming down from the left, to the right of a broad corrie. Turn south off the path and aim for this ridge. Once on the ridge the climbing is steep, and the ridge itself curves around to the southeast, high above the Red Glen.

A superb hill walk to the highest point on Hoy.

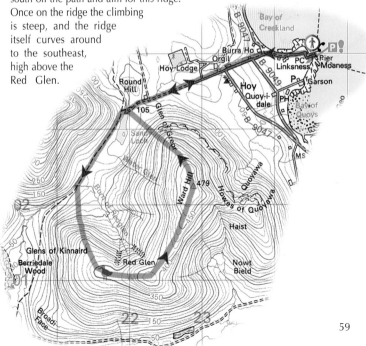

Wildflower meadows at Moaness below Ward Hill

As you gain height the gradient eases slightly, until you are on the broad ridge to the southwest of the summit of Ward Hill. Turn first east along the ridge, then northeast, climbing again now as you make for the summit of Ward Hill. The top has an OS trig pillar and is at 479m. This is the highest point in the whole of the Northern Isles.

From the summit head northwest down a steep ridge. As you drop down, veer off to the left slightly, aiming for Sandy Loch. The going is easier this way, as to continue down the ridge itself involves some loose rock.

Once at Sandy Loch walk around it anticlockwise, to the dam at the northern end. From this point, pick up the track and then the road back to Moaness.

NORTHERN ISLANDS

WALK 16

*Rousay – Knitchen Hill and Trumland
RSPB Reserve*

Start/finish	The ferry terminal at Trumland.
Grid ref	HY436275
Distance	4.8km/3 miles
Time	2–3 hours
Maps	OS Explorer 464; OS Landranger 5 or 6

Start by walking up the lane from the ferry terminal. Turn left at the first road junction, then continue along the lane uphill to another T-junction. Here turn right along the B9064. Walk beyond the woodlands of Trumland

A pleasant moorland walk onto the RSPB's Trumland Reserve on the island of Rousay.

Trumland and Blotchnie Fiold

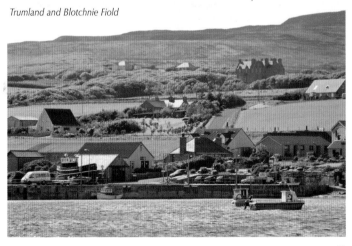

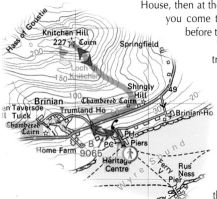

House, then at the next field boundary on the left you come to a track beside it. This is just before the house at Shingly Hill.

Turn off the road and follow the track to the northwest, climbing steeply at first, then coming to a flatter section of hillside. Here you reach a junction in the track. Turn right and follow the track up the ridge above, climbing above Loch of Knitchen to reach the summit of Knitchen Hill at 227m. There is an ancient cairn here, as well as the obligatory OS trig pillar.

The RSPB manages a large chunk of the moorland up here above Trumland. It's a wonderful place for wildlife, and you might see hunting merlin, hen harriers, or short-eared owls, as well as wheatears, meadow pipits, skylarks, ravens, golden plovers and curlews.

Return to the pier via the same route.

Trumland House on Rousay

WALK 17

Rousay – Mid Howe Broch and the Westness Walk

Start/finish	The car park overlooking the Mid Howe Broch.
Grid ref	HY376307
Distance	6.4km/4 miles
Time	2–3 hours
Maps	OS Explorer 464; OS Landranger 6

From the car park a path leads down the steep grassy hill to the southwest. Stay on the left side of the wall lower down, and soon pass through a gate to the left of a huge, green-roofed building.

A superb walk to two of the most impressive archaeological remains on Orkney.

The green-roofed building looks a little incongruous from above, but actually holds one of the real treasures of Orkney, the **Mid Howe Chambered Cairn**. It is the sheer size of the tomb that makes Mid Howe so impressive. It is 23m (75 feet) from one end to the other, and the central passageway through the tomb has stalls on either side. There is a walkway above the tomb, so you can look down into it and marvel at the work that went into building such a massive structure.

Go into the building (free) and walk through via the walkway. There is an exit door at the far end of the building, and once you have finished being impressed with the remarkable achievements of early man, go through the door to be confronted immediately by another spectacular structure.

Just a few metres along the coast behind the Mid Howe Cairn is the Mid Howe Broch, a fantastic 2000-year-old fortified dwelling place. All brochs are of a similar design, being double-walled, with a stairway between the walls that leads up to the higher floors.

The Mid Howe Broch

Walk back to the southeast, passing the Mid Howe Cairn's 'hut', and continue along the coast, picking up a path that leads through the sad and scattered remains of the various farmsteads of Skaill that once sat along the coast.

The farms at **Skaill** and **Swandro** have Norse origins, and there are many interpretation boards throughout the complex detailing what life would have been like here until fairly recently.

Continue along the coast to the lovely Bay of Westness, where you come to the present farm buildings at Westness itself.

There is a track to the left, climbing up between the barns to the east. Go up this and out beyond the farm-yard onto their driveway. Look for a track on the left. Take this and follow it northwestwards, running parallel to and between the coast below and the minor road above.

The track leads through fields and back to the path from the car park to the Mid Howe Cairn. Once you gain this track turn right and climb back uphill to your car.

WALK 18

Rousay – the Suso Burn and Kierfea Hill

Start/finish	Find a sensible place to park by the junction with the B9064 and the dead-end road leading up Brendale.
Grid ref	HY432317
Distance	7.7km/4.8 miles
Time	5–6 hours
Maps	OS Explorer 464; OS Landranger 5 or 6

From the car park walk northwestwards along the road until you come to a big bend to the left. Go around the bend and head west along the road until you pass through a wall at a cattle-grid. Turn off the road here and climb southwards, along the west side of the wall.

The way is steep, and some might say gruelling, but it is a short climb to the summit of Kierfea Hill, which lies quarter of a mile west of the wall and is obvious – it is a rounded dome marked by an ancient cairn and an OS trig point.

An invigorating walk to the summit of Kierfea Hill and on to the Suso Burn.

65

The summit height of **Kierfea Hill** seems to confuse a lot of people, the Ordnance Survey included. Their latest Explorer map shows the height of the hill as 235m, but then gives 236m in brackets!

The west ridge of Kierfea Hill is a wonderful place to stride out, if only for a short stretch. Head west along the ridge, admiring the fine views to the north to Westray and Papa Westray.

After a mile, descend to the southwest to the Loch of Withamo, from where the ridge below this pool continues to the southwest. Descend along the ridge for a short way, then aim off to the southeast, dropping into the valley holding the Suso Burn.

On the north side of this burn is a track. Turn left along the track and follow it out to the point where you've left your car, on the B9064.

WALK 19

Rousay – Faraclett Head

Start/finish	The small car park alongside the lane below the farm at Faraclett.
Grid ref	HY445323
Distance	3.7km/2.3 miles
Time	1–2 hours
Maps	OS Explorer 464; OS Landranger 5 or 6

This is a great moorland walk into the heart of prime nesting country for the great skua.

From the car park a path leads northwest to a stile over a fence. Climb the stile then bear right, to the north, following widely spaced waymarkers. Go through a stone wall, then onwards along a path to another stile high above the Loch of Scockness. Cross the stile and veer diagonally to the right, uphill.

The moorland here is a superb place to see **great skuas**, or **bonxies**. They nest in good numbers, and during the summer you will see plenty of these big brown seabirds. Also present up here are Arctic skuas, as well as wading birds such as snipe, oystercatchers, lapwings and golden plover.

The path is obvious and turns around the northern side of Faraclett Head, curving around to head west. Follow the path throughout, climbing with it up to the top of the hill itself. The views northwards from here are extensive, reaching as far as North Ronaldsay, Sandray, Westray and Papa Westray. On a very clear day you can see as far as Fair Isle, way off on the horizon.

The path now takes you southwest, along the high ground to a point where it suddenly swings to the left. Follow it down and along the south side of Faraclett Head, heading southeast.

Pass the remains of a chambered cairn, then reach a stone wall with a stile and a gate. Climb the stile and keep an eye out way over to the right for a post that marks the route down to your car.

WALK 20

Eday – Ward Hill and War Ness

Start/finish	Park at the southern end of a minor road running south from the roadside pub that stands on the bend of the B9063.
Grid ref	HY561289
Distance	3.9km/2.4 miles
Time	2–3 hours
Map	OS Explorer 465; OS Landranger 5 or 6

A walk to the spectacular viewpoint on Ward Hill, and around War Ness, the southern headland of the island of Eday.

Start at the small car park overlooking the lovely Bay of Greentoft, right at the south end of the island. Head west along the coast, passing the outflow from the Lady Well, the strongest spring on the island, producing 60 gallons of water per hour.

Follow the coast around to War Ness, the headland overlooking the islands of Muckle Green Holm and Little Green Holm, while common seals can be spotted nearer at hand on the flat rocks below the head.

Now the coast turns to the north, and you should follow it towards the rising cliffs below Ward Hill.

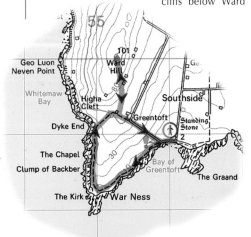

Wildflower meadows on Eday

The islands of **Muckle Green Holm** and **Little Green Holm** are important grey seal breeding grounds, where each autumn around 650 pups are born. The tidal race between Eday and the Holms is one of the strongest rips in the area. This, the Fall of Warness, has been chosen as a test site for the European Marine Energy Centre – making it the first of its kind in Europe.

As the cliffs rise you'll come to a bay backed by cliffs at Dyke End, and this is a good place to look out for puffins, as well as a host of wildflowers, including spring squill, thrift and lady's bedstraw.

The path veers away from the cliffs at Dyke End, heading northeastwards, and from this point you can tackle the south ridge of Ward Hill. It's only 45m (150) feet climbing to the top from here, but the views from the summit at 101m are amazing.

Head back down to the south to rejoin the path, and turn left along it to Greentoft Farm. At Greentoft take the track heading southeast, and this will lead you in half a mile to the Bay of Greentoft and the end of a lovely walk.

WALK 21
Eday – Noup Hill and Red Head

Start/finish	Park at the Setter Stone, just north of Mill Loch.
Grid ref	HY563371
Distance	8km/5 miles
Time	2–3 hours
Maps	OS Explorer 465; OS Landranger 5

A superb walk to the northern tip of this lovely island.

From the Setter Stone, just north of Mill Loch, walk northwards across a moor.

The **Setter Stone** is the tallest single monolith in the whole of the Northern Isles, at an impressive 4.5m.

The path leads across heathland to the Old School, then onwards past a number of chambered cairns.

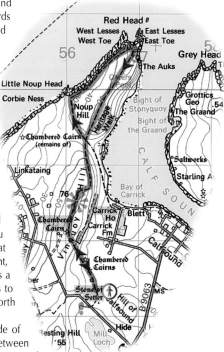

The chambered cairn at **Vinquoy Hill** has been restored and can be explored through a little gateway. It has four side chambers, and is thought to date from around 2000BC.

The way leads up and onto the south end of the ridge of Vinquoy Hill, and you should follow this ridge as it takes you to the northeast to the summit at 76m. Although of a lowly height, the summit of Vinquoy Hill is a magnificent viewpoint across to the islands of Sanday and North Ronaldsay.

Drop down the north side of the hill and into a little col between Vinquoy and Noup Hill. There is a path junction here, and you turn left for the coast at little Noup Head. Now turn right and follow the wonderfully craggy coastline to Red Head at the northern tip of the island.

Red Head supports breeding fulmars and rock doves, while the island to the east, the **Calf of Eday**, is home to large numbers of breeding puffins, razorbills, guillemots, shags and kittiwakes.

From the OS trig pillar on Red Head turn southwestwards along the spine of the ridge. This path leads over Noup Hill and down to the col that you passed earlier.

The Calf Sound lighthouse was built in 1909 by David Stevenson.

Look down to your left to see the lighthouse overlooking Calf Sound. ◄

Cross over the col and retrace your steps over Vinquoy Hill, perhaps wandering down to Mill Loch from the car-parking place to see if you can spot any red-throated divers.

Mill Loch has one of the largest concentrations of **nesting red-throated divers** in the UK. There is a bird hide here, which has been set up so as not to disturb these sensitive birds when they are on the nest.

Eday at sunset

WALK 22
Eday – Fers Ness and West Side

Start/finish	Park at the turn off to Fersness, on a bend in the minor road.
Grid ref	HY533333
Distance	7.2km/4.5 miles
Time	1–2 hours
Maps	OS Explorer 465; OS Landranger 5 or 6

Begin by walking northwestwards along the track from the car-parking spot, aiming for the farm at Fersness. The track swings down to the coast to the east as you approach the farm, and you should follow this to get good views out across Fersness Bay.

A short walk around the long western side of the island of Eday.

Now turn northwards and follow the coast to the tip of Fers Ness. The ground here is low-lying, though the shore is rocky. Turn around the headland and walk down the west side of the peninsula, passing the burnt mound at Coursan before reaching the little rocky bluff of Seal Skerry. Keep your eyes peeled for seals hauled out on the rocks here, and you might even see the odd otter if you are lucky.

The beaches to the east of Seal Skerry are lovely, and you should not miss the opportunity to stroll along the sands of Sealskerry Bay. At the eastern end of the bay, climb up and gain the minor road. Turn left and follow the lane back to your car.

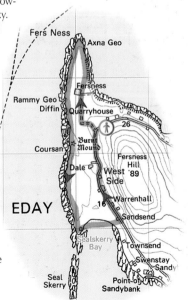

73

WALK 23

Westray – Inga Ness to Noup Head

Start	At the car park at East Kirbist
Grid ref	HY427437
Finish	At the car park at Noup Head
Grid ref	HY392498
Distance	17.2km /11 miles
Time	6–7 hours
Maps	OS Explorer 464; OS Landranger 5
Note	This route is linear, but it is easy to thumb a lift on these remote islands, so you'll have no problem getting back to your car.

Westray is the ideal place for a fantastic away-from-it-all walk, along the rough west side of the island.

From the car park at East Kirbist a path runs west to the farm at West Kirbist. Follow this, then continue out to the coast at Inga Ness. The path runs along the west side of the island, closely following the coast all the way, and you turn north along it, skirting around Skea Hill until you reach Whey Geo.

North of Whey Geo the coastal scenery is magnificent, and the route continues beneath the western flank of Fitty Hill. Do not deviate from the coast as you pass the small headland of Red Nev, then pass countless caves and natural arches in the cliffs as the route leads onwards, passing Neven o' Grinni, Starry Geo and Bis Geo.

Still the path leads the way, unerringly towards distant Noup Head. Fulmars soar past as you walk along the cliff tops, and if you keep an eye on the sea you might be lucky enough to spot dolphins or porpoise passing the headlands.

Tucked in under the cliff edge is Gentlemen's Cave, then a little further along, the caves of Lawrence's Piece, as you are forced inland around Ramni Geo.

Beyond Bis Geo the path takes you around the wild headlands of Bosan, then into the lovely little cove of Monivey Bay. Ahead rises North Hill, while the path sticks to the coast and passes to the left of this mound. ◄

This stunningly beautiful walk is almost over now, and a little further along the coast the lighthouse at Noup Head draws you in, beyond the fantastically named

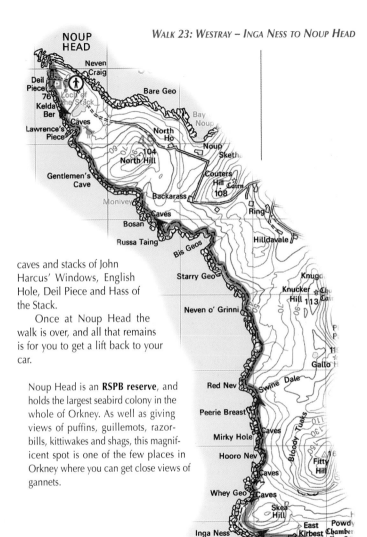

caves and stacks of John Harcus' Windows, English Hole, Deil Piece and Hass of the Stack.

Once at Noup Head the walk is over, and all that remains is for you to get a lift back to your car.

Noup Head is an **RSPB reserve**, and holds the largest seabird colony in the whole of Orkney. As well as giving views of puffins, guillemots, razorbills, kittiwakes and shags, this magnificent spot is one of the few places in Orkney where you can get close views of gannets.

A shag on the island of Papa Westray

WALK 24

*Papa Westray – Mull Head and the
North Hill RSPB Reserve*

Start/finish	At the small car park by Rose Cottage, where the road bends to the right at the entrance to the RSPB reserve.
Grid ref	HY495537
Distance	3.2km/2 miles
Time	2–3 hours
Maps	OS Explorer 464; OS Landranger 5

From the entrance to the nature reserve a path runs northwards towards a birdwatching hide. Follow the path, passing the Loch of Hyndgreenie on your right. Along the crest of the low hill there are a number of lochs, and the path passes close to these on its way to the summit of North Hill at 48m.

A fine walk on one of Orkney's wildest islands.

North Hill is managed as a reserve in partnership between the RSPB and Scottish Natural Heritage, along with local people. The low cliffs along the

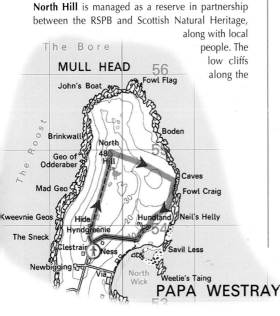

east coast are packed with seabirds during the nesting season, while the moorland of the interior has nesting Arctic terns and Arctic skuas. Lovers of wildflowers will also be delighted by the Scottish primroses that grow here.

Now walk eastwards, down towards the cliffs of Fowl Craig, one of the best places for Scottish primroses, and follow the waymarked trail southwards to Hundland. Here you pick up the end of the public road, and you follow this westwards to Gowrie, then on to the car park by the bend in the road.

The Scottish primrose

WALK 25

North Ronaldsay – Coastal traverse

Start/finish	At the pier at Nouster, at the southern end of North Ronaldsay.
Grid ref	HY750522
Distance	11.5km/7.2 miles
Time	4–5 hours
Maps	OS Explorer 465; OS Landranger 5

You don't have to be a serious birdwatcher to appreciate the wonderful scenery and away-from-it-all feel of the wild island of North Ronaldsay, although it is famous for the rare birds that turn up here on migration.

From the pier head go around the coast to the west, aiming for the flat rocks of the Lurn. Head north along the shore, picking your way over flat rocks and shingle, and passing close by beautiful Loch Gretchen. The route is never hard to find – just keep along the coast, and keep your eyes peeled for otters and seals!

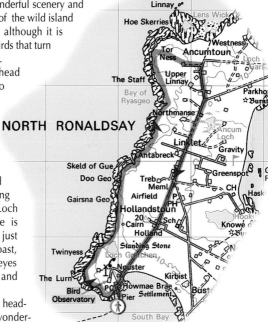

Round the broad headlands, where the wonderfully named Gairsna Geo and Doo Geo cut into Skeld of Gue, then continue towards the Bay of Ryasgeo. There are lots of

Wading birds are common here at Bay of Ryasgeo, and you should see turnstones, redshank, curlew, whimbrel, and of course the ever-present oystercatcher.

birds all along this shore, and it's also a good place to look for seals. ◄

Beyond Bay of Ryasgeo there is a slight rise and a sweeping headland – this is Tor Ness. Walk inland here, going eastwards towards the farm at Nether Linney. To the south of the farm is a track running eastwards, and if you aim for this you can follow it out to the minor road that runs the length of the island.

Turn right, southwards along the lane, and follow it down the island, through the scattered farms and houses at Linklet and on by the airstrip at Hollandstoun.

At the school in the hamlet of Holland you can look across the fields to the west and see the Ordnance Survey triangulation point that marks the highest 'hill' on North Ronaldsay. It is just 23m above sea level!

Continue along the lane to the southwest and you soon reach the pier at Nouster, overlooking the broad sands of South Bay.

SHETLAND

Fitful Head from Jarlshof (Walk 26)

SHETLAND (NORTH)

N

km
0   5   10

ATLANTIC OCEAN

76
77
75
Haroldswick
74
Baltasound
73 *Unst*
72
71
66
Fetlar 80
North Roe
65
79
YELL SOUND
Yell
78
COLGRAVE SOUND
64
70
Esha Ness
63
Ulsta
69
Hillswick
62
68
Sullom
Out Skerries
60
ST MAGNUS BAY
61
Muckle Roe
67
Laxo
Papa Stour
58
Symbister
59
52
Whalsay
50
51
49
47
NORTH SEA
Walls
48
45
Bressay
46
Lerwick
43
56
57 *Isle of Noss*

WALKING ON SHETLAND

The islands that make up Shetland are the further reaches northwards of the British Isles. They lie far out in the North Atlantic, geographically and historically closer to Norway than to Scotland.

The main island of this group is Mainland, which stretches in a rough north–south direction. This over-simplifies things, however, as there are hundreds of miles of coastline to discover on Mainland, with lots of huge headlands cut by beautiful long fjord-like seaways. The southern tip of Mainland is Sumburgh Head, while the northern point is the Point of Fethaland.

SHETLAND (SOUTH)

There are dozens of islands off Mainland, with Hermaness on Unst being the most northerly point that you can reach in the Shetland group. Only the rocky skerries of Muckle Flugga and Out Stack lie further north. South and west of Unst are the islands of Fetlar and Yell, both as wonderful as Unst itself and well worth exploring on foot.

Moving down the east side of Mainland, Whalsay lies just offshore, while the Out Skerries are very remote. Further south still, and just across the way from the capital of the islands, Lerwick, there is another large island, Bressay, with Noss – a national nature reserve – on its seaward side.

Further still down the east coast is the wonderfully idyllic island of Mousa, with its famous broch and equally famous wildlife!

Moving down the west side of Mainland from Fethaland in the north, the first big island is Muckle Roe, now connected to Mainland by a causeway, but nevertheless a superb place to explore. Other islands on this wild coast include Vementry, Papa Stour and Vaila, while way out to the west is desolate yet magnificent Foula.

Closer in and just south of the second town of the Shetlands, Scalloway, lie the islands of Trondra and East and West Burra, all again connected by causeways to Mainland. St Ninian's Isle deserves a mention here too. It lies south of Scalloway, just offshore from the little village of Bigton. St Ninian's Isle is famous for

being connected to Mainland by a 'tombolo' – a narrow spit of sand.

And finally, the last (or first, depending on where you start!) island in the group – lovely Fair Isle. This lonely outlier is found roughly midway between Sumburgh Head on the southern tip of Shetland Mainland and the low island of North Ronaldsay, the northeasterly island in the Orkney group.

Generally speaking, the islands of Shetland are wild and rugged at their hearts. Most have heather moorland falling away at the coasts to a strip of farmland, before dropping sharply down cliffs into the sea. It is this bleakness that makes Shetland such a grand place for a walking holiday, and it is this that sets it apart from most of the walking on Orkney.

Getting There

Fly to Sumburgh, the main airport in the Shetlands, from Inverness or Aberdeen. Contact British Airways and their franchise partners Logan Air on 0845 7733377 for flight information, www.loganair.co.uk.

North Link Ferries runs car ferries to Lerwick from either Aberdeen or Stromness (Orkney), tel 0845 6000 449, www.northlinkferries.co.uk.

Getting Around

Public transport does exist, but can be infrequent and irregular. It's probably best to either bring your own car on the ferry, or hire one once you arrive. For car hire, try either Bolts Car Hire

Loch o' Spiggie at sunset (Walk 29)

on 01595 693636, or Star Rent-a-Car on 01595 692075. Both have offices in Lerwick and at Sumburgh Airport.

Inter-island ferries on Shetland are run by the Shetland Islands Council and are very good indeed. In fact, recently the ferries running across the Bluemull Sound, between Yell, Unst and Fetlar, were made free of charge! For details of inter-island ferries contact 01595 743970, www.shetland.gov.uk/ferries.

The island of Mousa is best reached via the private boat Solan IV. This is owned by Tom Jamieson, who runs a regular service out to the island, www.mousaboattrips.co.uk, tel 01950 431367.

Where to Stay

There are a couple of places to stay that I would personally recommend on Shetland: Busta House near Brae, tel 01806 522506, www.busta house.com; and Almara Guesthouse in Upper Urafirth, Hillswick, North Mavine, tel 01595 503261, e-mail almara@zetnet.co.uk.

There are lots of other good options, and the best bet is to contact the tourist office in Lerwick (see below).

Other options include camping, and on Shetland wild camping is encouraged, although there there are also a few official campsites.

Enjoying the views out to Sumburgh Head from the Ness of Burgi (Walk 27)

The Tombolo at St Ninian's Isle (Walk 30)

- Clickimin Caravan and Campsite,
  tel 01595 741000,
  www.srt.org.uk.

- Levenwick Campsite,
  tel 01950 422207.

- Braewick Campsite,
  tel 01806 503345,
  www.eshaness.shetland.co.uk.

- Westings Inn Campsite,
  tel 01595 840242,
  www.originart.eu/westings.

- Skeld Caravan Site,
  tel 01595 860 287.

Tourist Information Office
There is an excellent TIC in the Market
Cross in Lerwick, tel 01595 693434,
www.visitshetland.com.

Useful Books
The Shetland Guidebook by Charles Tait.
Isles of the North by Ian Mitchell.
The Birds of Shetland by Pennington, Osborn, Harvey, Riddington, Okill, Ellis and Heubeck.
A Naturalist's Shetland by J Laughton Johnston.
The Islands of Scotland by Hamish Haswell Smith.
Backpacker's Britain, Vol 3: Northern Scotland by Graham Uney.

Wheelhouses at Jarlshof

MAINLAND SOUTH

WALK 26
Jarlshof and Sumburgh Head

Start/finish	Park at Sumburgh Hotel. Follow the A970 south from Lerwick, continuing to Sumburgh airport. Cross over the runway and take the long bend to the left, beyond Scatness. There is a turn off to the right, signposted for Jarlshof. Take this to the hotel car park, which is also used by Historic Scotland for those visiting Jarlshof.
Grid ref	HU399095
Distance	4km/2.5 miles
Time	2–3 hours
Maps	OS Explorer 466; OS Landranger 4

JARLSHOF

What remains at Jarlshof today emerged from beneath a huge sand dune during a magnificent storm in 1905. There are lots of interesting layers to Jarlshof, with its history spanning a period of over 4000 years. Viking remains are built on top of Pictish, which in turn are built on top of Iron Age, Bronze Age and Stone Age dwellings. The whole thing is topped by a 16th-century laird's mansion. The impressive wheelhouses are great fun to discover, as are the souterrains that can be explored beneath the ruins. The one thing that is false about Jarlshof is the name itself – it was invented by Sir Walter Scott in his novel The Pirate. There is a charge for entry, and coffee is available at the nearby hotel.

From the site, head around the front of the hotel and follow the road round to the right. This passes through a gate and takes you up to a farm. Go through the farmyard and out onto a narrow minor road. Turn right here and follow the road until you are beyond the roadside fences and out onto open grassy moorland.

Jarlshof is the single most important archaeological site in Shetland, and a fun place to begin or end this walk.

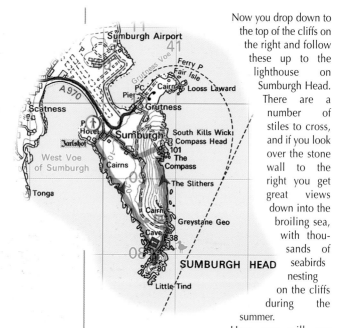

Now you drop down to the top of the cliffs on the right and follow these up to the lighthouse on Sumburgh Head. There are a number of stiles to cross, and if you look over the stone wall to the right you get great views down into the broiling sea, with thousands of seabirds nesting on the cliffs during the summer.

The lighthouse was built by the Stevenson family in 1821 and was the first to be built in Shetland.

Here you will see puffins, guillemots, razorbills, fulmar, kittiwakes, shags and rock doves, with occasional gannets and great skuas (known locally as bonxies) passing out to sea. Also in the summer you might see grey and common seals, as well as possibly a passing Minke whale or orca. Once up at the lighthouse there are viewing platforms provided by the RSPB. ◄

Follow the road down to a large car-parking area, looking for a huge whale bone as you go. Now, keeping to the cliff edge on the right, climb up over grass to the summit of the Compass. Pass to the right of the radar buildings, then follow the access road down to rejoin your outward route just above the Sumburgh Hotel.

At the junction turn left, then go right, back through the farmyard to return to the car park at the hotel.

Stone wall at Sumburgh Head

WALK 27

The Ness of Burgi Iron Age Fort

Start/finish	Park sensibly in Scatness village. Drive south on the A970 from Lerwick, towards Sumburgh Head. Pass over Sumburgh Airport runway and the Old Scatness Broch. Just beyond this the road bends to the left, and here, on the right, is a turn-off for Scatness village. Drive down this lane and park on the right before the turning circle at the end of the road.
Grid ref	HU388097
Distance	3.25km/2 miles
Time	1–2 hours
Maps	OS Explorer 466; OS Landranger 4

A short wildlife walk to a fascinating Iron Age fort.

From the small car-parking area walk southwards down the road to the car-turning bay. Go through a gate beside a house straight ahead and walk out into the open fields of Scatness. A lovely grassy path leads through the ancient field systems, taking you to a bouldery neck of land at the Hog of Breigeo. Here coastal erosion has eaten into the grassy sward from both sides.

Walk over the boulders to continue on grass to another very narrow neck of rocky ground. A path has

The scramble out to the Ness of Burgi

been constructed across this, and to the left side there is a handrail for those of a nervous disposition. Walk over the rocky ridge onto the Ness of Burgi.

Follow a little path over the short-cropped turf to the Ness of Burgi Iron Age fort.

Fitful head from Scatness

The **Ness of Burgi** Iron Age fort is a low, fortified dwelling place standing on a rocky promontory on the east side of the headland. You can walk through the twin ditches and up to the house, then crawl into the rooms by low doorways.

From the fort look down onto the seaward side and you may get a view of grey seals basking on the rocks below. The view out to the east is dominated by Sumburgh Head, while far out to the southwest you can see the hilly land of Fair Isle.

Once you've explored around the ness, return to your car by the same route.

93

WALK 28
Fitful Head

Start/finish	Park at Quendale Mill at the end of the minor road heading south from the halmet of Quendale. Follow signs for the mill from the main A970. Park sensibly here, or ask for permission to park at the mill itself.
Grid ref	HU371133
Distance	9km/5.5 miles
Time	4–5 hours
Maps	OS Explorer 466; OS Landranger 4
Note	Map and compass skills required.

The dominating mass of Fitful Head makes for a superb walk on the southern half of Mainland.

Fitful Head

Start by heading north back along the lane from Quendale Mill. Just beyond Gord Farm, before you reach the Hillwell junction, you'll see a track on the left. Follow this easily up hill, heading westwards with the bold slopes of Fitful Head dead ahead.

Drop down a short way into the Black Meadow, where snipe, curlew, skylark and meadow pipits nest,

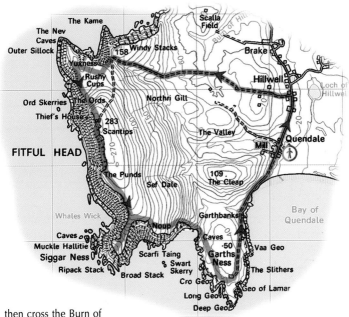

then cross the Burn of
Hillwell, before climbing again,
this time to a small group of sheep pens.

The track now passes out of the meadows and onto the
open hillside, making for a col between Windy Stacks
and Rushy Cups.

Continue along the track on the north side of the
Burn of Hillwell, which finds its source just below this
col. As you approach the col you'll notice that the track
takes a sharp turn to the left, and here you'll begin to get
the whiff of the sea in your nostrils.

The view down the west side of the col is of the sea,
where a broad cove between the Kame and the Nev
broils below you.

Walk westwards, away from the track, dropping
slightly then climbing to Yuxness. Climb steadily now to
the summit of Fitful Head at 283m. The top is marked by a
radar station 'golfball', and an OS trig pillar over a fence.

95

Fitful Head from Loch o' Spiggie

From the trig pillar head southwards over Scantips, keeping the fence to your right as you descend. You can make a detour out to Siggar Ness if you wish, but this does involve a descent of 70m, all of which would have to be regained before you can continue. However, the views down into Whales Wick on the right more than compensate for this, and you also get superb views southwards towards Fair Isle.

Down on the right is where **the Braer oil tanker** ran aground in 1993. This American-owned, Liberian-registered vessel foundered on Swart Skerry in the middle of Garth Wick to the east of Siggar Ness, spewing 85,000 tons of crude oil into the bay.

From the top of the Siggar Ness ridge turn eastwards, and continue alongside the fence to descend to the Noup. Here the views down into Garth Wick are superb, and the blue sea below certainly appears healthy enough to the untrained eye.

Below the Noup, where the Burn of Garth empties into the sea, you'll reach a track that cuts off Garths Ness at its neck. Follow this track northeastwards to Corston, then back northwards above the beautiful Bay of Quendale to Quendale Mill.

WALK 29
Around Fora Ness

Start/finish	Park on the Scousburgh Dunes overlooking the Bay of Scousburgh. To get there, turn westwards down the hill in South Scousburgh, passing the Spiggie Hotel, and continue to the northern end of Loch o' Spiggie. Here you'll see a signpost pointing north to the beach.
Grid ref	HU372179
Distance	5km/3 miles
Time	2–3 hours
Maps	OS Explorer 466; OS Landranger 4

From the dunes head down to the shore and follow the lovely beach westwards onto the headland that forms its western arm.

A short coastal walk around the headlands of the Moul and Fora Ness.

Look for divers fishing in the bay, while fulmar skim the cliff edges as you walk along the coast to **the Moul**. From the Moul the views northwards take in wonderful St Ninian's Isle, with its impressive tombolo, and to the northwest the small islet of Colsay.

Follow the cliff tops around the Moul, skirting around Muckle Sound, where grey seals bask just off shore. You soon reach the Orms, and here the easiest way to

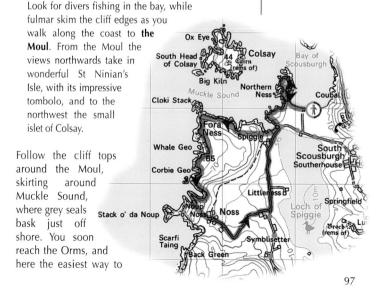

97

proceed is to drop down to the tiny beach, then hop over a little channel to gain the cliff tops again, just north of the farm at Spiggie.

Now, open grassy moorland forms the main vegetation as you walk westwards to the lower point of Fora Ness at its northwestern extreme. Here you are looking down on the broken skerries of Cloki Stack. Now turn southwards along the cliff tops to gain the highest point of Fora Ness, known as Gilden's Get, a small plateau perched above the deep cleft of Whale Geo.

The route southwards is obvious if you stay close to the cliff tops. You skim around another large geo, then can make your way out to the headland of Noup o' Ness, from where you can gaze out at the remarkable arête formed by the Stack o' da Noup.

Fulmars scythe the air, while out at sea, gannets fish in deeper waters. You should also look for shags here, down at the base of the cliffs.

Loch o' Spiggie

Head southeastwards along the cliffs to the northern fringe of another geo, then inland to where you can pick

up a track to the farm and road end at Noss. Follow the
road out to a T-junction overlooking Loch o' Spiggie.

*Fitful Head from
Loch o' Spiggie
in winter*

Loch o' Spiggie is an important over-wintering site for
thousands of birds, including ducks, geese and hundreds of whooper swans. The RSPB maintains a small
information hut here on the northern side of the loch,
and also keeps an eye on the many nesting birds that
use the site during the summer.

Turn left at the junction and follow the road to the northern end of the loch, where you can pick up the track
leading down to your car on the dunes.

WALK 30

St Ninian's Isle over the tombolo

Start/finish	Car park below the village of Bigton. Follow the A970 south from Lerwick and turn right onto the B9122 on the big bend just beyond Channerwick. Follow signs for Bigton, and where the road swings sharply to the right in the village, turn left and follow the track down to the car park just above the beach.
Grid ref	HU374208
Distance	5km/3 miles
Time	2–3 hours
Maps	OS Explorer 466; OS Landranger 4

A unique opportunity to walk over a tombolo to a stunning island.

From the car park at the bottom of the track, cross the tombolo, keeping an eye out for nesting terns.

Terns are delightful, light-winged birds, but they will soon let you know if you get too close during the nesting season – if you start being dive-bombed, move away quickly!

Once over the tombolo follow the path up to the left through marram grass dunes. Keep left along the top of the cliffs overlooking St Ninian's Bay, and soon there are superb views over the small islets of Coar Holm and Inns Holm, with the imposing outline of Fitful Head in the distance, beyond Colsay.

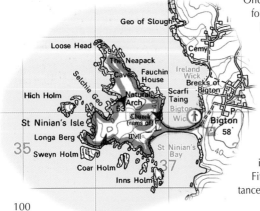

ST NINIAN'S ISLE

St Ninian's Isle is named after a 12th-century church which you can explore the remains of at the end of this delightful walk. Many historians believe that the site was used as a domestic residence from the 1st century BC, and then as a pre-Christian burial ground from the 3rd century AD. Christian burials began here soon after this period, and Norse settlers on the island built a larger chapel on the site of the first. This was enlarged during the 12th century, but when the population left the island in the 1700s, this chapel became a ruin. The ruin that we see today was excavated in the 1950s, as it had become buried under wind-driven sand. During the excavation a local schoolboy unearthed the remains of a larch-wood box. It contained 28 pieces of Pictish silver, which are now on display at the Royal Museum in Edinburgh.

The once-tidal island of St Ninian's Isle is linked to Mainland at Bigton by an isthmus of lovely white shell-sand, known as a tombolo. Dunes of machair lead onto the tombolo, which is composed of a deep layer of sand lying on top of a spit of shingle. This sand makes the St Ninian's Isle tombolo unique in Britain – elsewhere they are composed purely of shingle or gravel.

Exploring St Ninian's Isle

Walking towards the tombolo on St Ninian's Isle

Continuing around the island in a clockwise direction, you soon reach a stone wall. Follow this up the hill to pass through a gate. Turn back to the cliffs and follow them onwards.

Keep an eye open for **grey seals** on the westward side of the isle, particularly around Sweyn Holm and Longa Berg. From Longa Berg there's a great view over the huge expanse of ocean, with the lonely island of Foula way out on the horizon. Further along the coast you might see kittiwakes, fulmars, and perhaps a few puffins at Selchie Geo.

Onwards you reach Loose Head, where you turn southeastwards to the stone wall. Follow it rightwards to a gate, from where an easy stroll eastwards takes you to the remains of the chapel. Cross back over the tombolo to the car park.

WALK 31

To the Taing of Maywick

Start/finish	Park sensibly at the end of the road in Maywick.
Grid ref	HU377246
Distance	1.5km/1 mile
Time	1 hour
Maps	OS Explorer 466; OS Landranger 4

At the end of the public lane, where it swings off to the left, follow the track out onto the rough meadows above the houses of the hamlet. Once clear of the hamlet, follow a fence westwards,

This is a short stroll around the bay of May Wick to the headland that forms its western arm.

The coast near Maywick at sunset (Walk 32)

going uphill to a lovely little lochan. Snipe call from the top of fenceposts during the breeding season, and you might see red-throated divers fishing on the lochan.

Now head north out onto the Taing of Maywick, watching as fulmars brush the cliff edges with their stiff wings. Grey seals often bob in the bay, and if you're really lucky you might catch a glimpse of an otter here too.

You can return the same way, or follow the cliff top around to the southwest a short way, following a fence back to the lochan before descending to Maywick.

WALK 32

Deepdale from Maywick

Start/finish	Park sensibly at the end of the road in Maywick.
Grid ref	HU377246
Distance	9.5km/6 miles
Time	4–5 hours
Maps	OS Explorer 466; OS Landranger 4

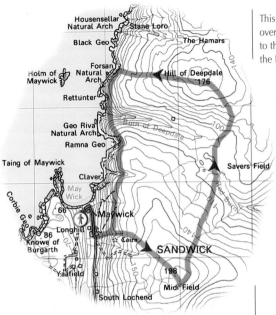

This is a wild walk over rough moorland to the northeast of the Dale of Maywick.

From Maywick walk back along the road heading southwards until you reach the bend at Longhill. Walk around the bend, then, within 100m, you'll see a track on the left heading steeply uphill. Follow this, initially to the southeast, then to the northeast, to where it emerges from the confines of the dale onto the open moorland of Midi Field.

Continue uphill on the track, between the Burn of Vadsgill to the south and the Burn of Pundsgill to the north. When the track ends, continue southeastwards over rough moorland to the summit of Midi Field at 198m. ▶

Turn northwards down the broad slopes of the hill, descending to Red Burn, then continuing up the other side to Savers Field – a broad southeast ridge of Hill of Deepdale. The views down into the lonely depths of Deepdale to the west from here show it to be a wild and little-visited place.

The moorland here supports a few red grouse, as well as dunlin, curlew and snipe. You might also be lucky enough to spot a dashing merlin hunting over the heather.

105

Follow the ridge of Savers Field around to the north-west, climbing steadily to the fine summit of Hill of Deepdale at 176m. The highest point is known, unfathomably, as Erne's Toug.

Now drop down westwards towards the west coast overlooking Holm of Maywick. Pass three lochans on the western flank of the hill, and soon find yourself at the upper end of the fine geo of Forsan. Turn southwards along the coast, keeping an eye out for a superb natural arch where kittiwakes nest and black guillemots, or tysties, can also be seen.

Drop down now, alongside the cliffs, into Deepdale. You should wander up the dale, following the burn for a short way to a small but fine waterfall.

Head southwestwards uphill, back to the cliffs, to Ramna Geo, a superb natural amphitheatre of wheeling birds and boiling waters. A fence runs along the cliff tops here, and you should follow this southwards, crossing the Burn of Claver, before dropping down beside the Burn of Seagill back to the end of the road in Maywick.

Sandwick and No Ness (Walk 33)

WALK 33

Sandwick to No Ness

Start/finish	Park in Sandwick village, at the eastern end of the bay where the road bends sharply to the southeast.
Grid ref	HU436236
Distance	6.5km /4 miles
Time	2–3 hours
Maps	OS Explorer 466; OS Landranger 4

Begin by striding out along the lane southwards, keeping Sand Wick to your right as you go. The lane leads through pastures, where skylarks and meadow pipits sing, to Curefield, and just beyond you come to the farm at Noness.

The way continues southwards as a track at first, then, as this gives way to close-cropped grass, it's a simple matter of finding your own route around the low cliff tops. Make sure you do not wander too far from the cliffs, however, as the natural arches and caves at Skaag and Vins Taing are well worth seeing.

Right at the end of the peninsula, where the cliffs reach their high point, there is a fine sea stack known as Stack of Billyageo. Just back from the cliff edge here you'll see the Loch of Noness, where you might spot

The delightful village of Sandwick is a great place to start a walk. The bay is one of the most beautiful on the east coast of Mainland, and this walk gives fine views across its levels.

Walk across the Tombolo to St Ninian's Isle (Walk 30)

red-throated divers, or perhaps snipe and dunlin feeding in the shallows.

Now, as you round the peninsula and begin the walk back northwards, the way leads around superb Muckle Brei Geo, then out to the small headland of Holpur. Corbie Geo is the next small cove to be reached, and then 500m further north is the large rocky gulf of Lagars Geo.

From where this void is sliced out of the cliffs it's a short stroll westwards to the farm at Noness, so if you want to cut your walk short, now's the time. It's best, however, to continue around the wild headland of Hoga, where you'll find the remains of an ancient dwelling place, the Broch of Burraland. This lies in a superb position on a narrow neck of land connecting the headland of Hoga to Mainland. The conical building, probably dating back 2000 years, overlooks the more substantial and impressive broch on Mousa just across the sound to the east.

From the Broch of Burraland head northwest, diagonally away from the coast now, towards the low hill of Ward of Burraland. Here, on the eastern side of the hill, you come across a track that leads northwards.

At a junction in the track turn left to Pund, where you hit a tarmac lane. Now turn right and follow the lane around a bend to the left to another junction. Turn left at this T-junction and follow the lane into Sandwick.

WALK 34

The Helli Ness Peninsula

Start/finish	Park sensibly at Greenmow on the east side of Aith Voe.
Grid ref	HU444289
Distance	4.8km/3 miles
Time	2 hours
Maps	OS Explorer 466; OS Landranger 4

From Greenmow walk along the lane southwards to Aness. As you approach the buildings at the road end, bear eastwards down to the coast. Walk eastwards beneath the Ward of Greenmow, the low hill to the north, keeping an eye out for otters along the shore as you go.

A short coastal walk out to this fine headland, giving superb views down to the island of Mousa, and northeastwards towards Bressay and Noss.

The **otters** found on the coast here are the same species as those found on rivers in mainland Britain. Many people mistakenly believe that we have two species, the river otter and the sea otter, but the same species lives a different kind of life accord-

ing to its territory. On rivers, otters tend to be mainly nocturnal, whereas by the sea they seem to prefer to hunt on a rising tide, which makes them easier to spot during the day. Even those otters that live by the coast

109

need fresh water though, as they have to wash salt from their coats to retain the coat's insulating properties.

Beyond the Holm of Helliness there is a long peninsula jutting out to the southeast, and you can walk right out along this to gain fine views over Dedda Skerry, where grey seals often bask on sunny days.

Now head north, passing the Taing of Helliness to the headland of Helli Ness itself. There is an Ordnance Survey trig pillar here at 39m above the sea. Just on the north side of the headland is wonderful Uxna Geo, a deep voe cutting into the cliffs. Beyond this the coast turns back towards the west, and you should follow it past Turri Ness and round into a little bay.

Now leave the coast and head southwestwards, climbing slightly to a couple of prominent boulders known as the Grey Stanes. At the top of this little ridge there is a view down the other side to Greenmow, and a short stroll will return you to your vehicle.

WALK 35

Muskna Field from Wester Quarff

Start/finish	Park sensibly at Wester Quarff, on the south side of the valley near Beneath-a-Burn.
Grid ref	HU407347
Distance	5.6km/3.5 miles
Time	2 hours
Maps	OS Explorer 466; OS Landranger 4

A walk to one of the more prominent hills of South Mainland, giving great views westwards to the islands of Burra and Trondra.

Start by walking westwards along the road, on the south side of the valley, until you are above the West Voe of Quarff. At the end of the road, by some private houses at the ness, head uphill to the south, gaining the open moorland at Bogabreck.

Climb straight up the easy-angled north ridge of Muskna Field, enjoying the fine views down into Clift

Sound to the west and the Glen of Quarff to the east. The ridge soon levels out, and you find the summit of Muskna Field to be a broad plateau of heather moorland. The summit of Muskna Field lies at the southern end at 262m and is marked by a small cairn.

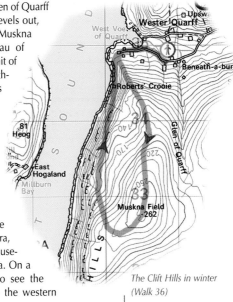

Now head southwest for half a mile, to the top edge of the cliffs known as Clift Hills. The views from here are impressive, as the hill sweeps down into the long narrow channel of Clift Sound below you. Across the sound are the islands of East and West Burra, adjoined to Mainland via causeways leading over to Trondra. On a clear day you'll be able to see the island of Foula way off on the western

The Clift Hills in winter (Walk 36)

horizon. Eastwards the coast of Mainland is clearly visible too, and to the northeast, over the top of Sheens of Breitoe (224m), the highest point of the island of Bressay, Ward Hill, can be seen.

Now head north along the Clift Hills, dropping down into a broad bowl known as Quirills Dale. Stay on the easy ground, keeping the steep, broken flank falling into Clift Sound close by to your left. Soon you find yourself descending back to the ness, and the end of the lane at Wester Quarff.

WALK 36
Scrae Field and the White Stone of Toufield

Start/finish	Park at Easterhoull, just south of the road junction that leads over the causeway to the island of Trondra.
Grid ref	HU407383
Distance	9.6km/6 miles
Time	3–4 hours
Maps	OS Explorer 466; OS Landranger 4
Note	Map and compass skills required.

A fine hill walk, giving extensive views westwards to distant Foula.

Note There is a path coming up from Wester Quarff, and this gives a good alternative route of ascent.

Start by walking south along the lane to Uradale. At Uradale pick up a path that initially runs along the east bank of the Burn of Sundibanks. This path soon crosses over to the west bank and leads you on a gentle climb southwards, up the ridge of the Kame of Whalwick. The views from here, out westwards over Trondra towards distant Foula, are tremendous.

Continue down the south side of the Kame of Whalwick into a little col, where the path veers off southeastwards, then south and down into Wester Quarff. Before you begin to drop downhill towards this little village, however, you should turn to the east and climb steeply up the southeastern flank of Scrae Field. ◄

Climb this southwest ridge of Scrae Field, known as North Snuckle, then follow the rising ground northwards to the OS trig pillar at the summit of Scrae Field (216m).

The ridge running northwards from the summit leads easily down into a col above the lovely hidden Loch of Couster.

> Loch of Couster is a good place to see **red-throated divers**. These large, spectacular birds nest on high lochs in the moors and hills, although in bad weather they are most often seen fishing close to the coast on sea lochs. This behaviour has given them the local name 'rain geese'.

Continue northwards to an angle in a fence at the White Stone of Toufield. Now drop down the hillside to the northwest, aiming for the road end at Uradale. Keep to the left of the fence that cuts diagonally down the hill and soon reach the track in the dale bottom. Turn northwards and retrace your steps to your car.

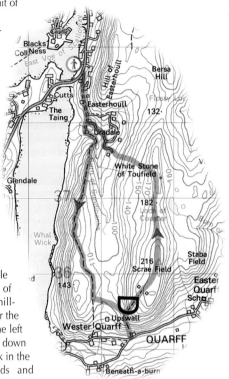

Ward Hill from the sea

SOUTHERN ISLANDS

WALK 37
Fair Isle – the Climb to Ward Hill

Start/finish	At the junction of the track leading to the landing strip, a mile southwest along the lane from the ferry pier in North Haven.
Grid ref	HZ212717
Distance	5.6km/3.5 miles (8.8km/5.5 miles from the pier in North Haven)
Time	2 hours
Maps	OS Explorer 466; OS Landranger 4

A short walk to the highest point on Fair Isle. There are many corners to explore on this magical island, but for those with limited time this is as good a walk as any.

Note The longer walk along the West Coast traverse (Walk 39) incorporates the climb up to Ward Hill.

Start by heading north across the landing strip. There is a track here that goes up to an aerial on the east side of the hill. Soon after crossing the landing strip look for a path on the right, running northeastwards. Follow this, climbing at first, then contouring around the east side of Ward Hill.

The path turns to the northwest, and eventually leads around to the north side of Ward Hill. You should turn southwards here and climb steeply up to the summit at 217m, where you'll find an Ordnance Survey trig pillar.

The views from the top of **Ward Hill** on a clear day are magical. You can see Sumburgh Head on the southern tip of Shetland Mainland, 40km (24 miles) away to the northeast, and the low-lying Orkney islands of North Ronaldsay, Sanday and Papa Westray a similar distance away to the southwest.

Descend to the south along a vague ridge, veering off slightly to the west to get great views down into the deep and rocky coves of the west side. Now turn eastwards to gain the track that runs up the hill from the landing strip. Turn southwards along this to return to the starting point.

The Nizz
Cristal Kame
Skroo
Natural Arches
Stacks of Skroo
Saaversteen
Ferry P
Grutness
Dronger
Milens
houllan
92
Mopul
North Fellsigeo
Wirrvie
Brecks
Ward
Hill
Caves
Stacks of Wirrvie
Heads of Peitron
Tower of Ward Hill
217
Ler Ness
Swey
North Naaversgill
Brae of
Restensgeo
Furse
North Gavel
Cave
Burrista
Eas
Brecks
Burnt
Mounds
Breiti Stack
Bird Obsy
Pier
Bu Ness
Burrashield
Hoiliff
Colsta
Burnt
Mound
Landing
Strip
N. Haven
S. Haven
fort
8
Muckle Geo of Hoini
Hoini
South Gavel
Kista
Burnt Mound
Hundi Stack
Pund
Vaasetter
04
FAIR ISLE

Birdwatching on
Fair Isle

WALK 38

Fair Isle – Malcolm's Head

Start/finish	At the telephone box at Shirva, 3km (2 miles) southwest along the lane from the ferry pier in North Haven – turn left along the western road on the island, passing Stonybreck.
Grid ref	HZ203706
Distance	2.9km/1.8 miles (9.3km/5.8 miles from the pier in North Haven)
Time	1 hour
Maps	OS Explorer 466; OS Landranger 4

A superb coastal walk out to the southwestern tip of Fair Isle. The longer walk along the West Coast traverse (Walk 39) incorporates this section of coastline.

From the telephone box at Shirva, start by heading west out to the cliffs in the big natural bay overlooking Malcolm's Head. Turn southwards and follow the cliffs to a deep gully, where the coastline swings away to the northwest, and the climb up to Malcolm's Head begins. The going is steady, and the views northwards along the west coast of the island are incredible.

Malcolm's Head summit is at 107m above sea level, and a superb place to watch both seabirds passing, and on the cliffs themselves during the nesting season. You should be able to spot fulmars, kittiwakes, guillemots,

An Arctic tern on Fair Isle

black guillemots, razorbills, puffins, rock doves and shags here.

Head right out to the westernmost tip of Malcolm's Head, then walk southwards downhill alongside the cliff edge. Keep an eye out for the big natural stone arches that grace this section of coastline, and seals can be seen basking on the skerries of the Crivv.

As you descend further you come to a big rocky cleft at Mathers Head. Here there is a small jetty, and at this point you should head eastwards, inland, to the road near Haa. Turn northwards to return along the road to Shirva.

WALK 39

Fair Isle – A West Coast traverse

Start/finish	The ferry pier in North Haven.
Grid ref	HZ225725
Distance	16km/10 miles
Time	8 hours
Maps	OS Explorer 466; OS Landranger 4
Note	Map and compass skills required.

Start from the pier in North Haven and follow the lane westwards to the bird observatory. At the junction just beyond this, turn right and follow the lane northwestwards, until it bends sharply to the right above Furse. Now leave the road and climb northwestwards, over rough grassy moorland, reaching a track that skirts around the eastern flank of Ward Hill.

A fantastic walk along the entire west coast of Fair Isle.

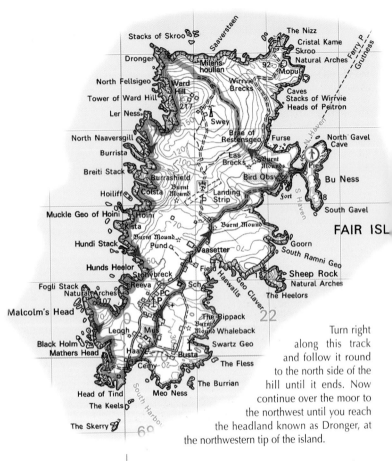

Turn right along this track and follow it round to the north side of the hill until it ends. Now continue over the moor to the northwest until you reach the headland known as Dronger, at the northwestern tip of the island.

The views from **Dronger** along the north coast stretching eastwards, and the west coast stretching southwards, are very impressive, taking in some of the finest rock scenery to be found anywhere in Britain.

Turn southwards along the cliff-top edge, watching in awe as fulmars scythe through the air and lots of auks come and go below you. Throughout this walk the idea is to keep as close to the cliff edge as you can, taking in all the deep-cut geos and headlands as you go. However, the summit of Ward Hill lies only a short way back from the edge, and unless you've already climbed it, you may as well detour slightly to reach the highest point of the island at 217m.

Just north of west from Ward Hill is the spectacular Tower of Ward Hill, a huge sloping fang of rock barely attached to the main island. From here, head south along the coastline, passing around a huge gulf as you swing to the west to gain the headland of Ler Ness.

Just south of Ler Ness is the yawning channel of North Naaversgill, which cuts deeply into the land mass. On the south side of this there is a wonderful natural arch that is worth seeking out.

Continue around the coast, passing to the west of the small hill of Burrashield, then dropping down to

Walking on Fair Isle

another remarkable narrow cleft in the cliffs below. This is a good place to see nesting shags and black guillemots. Pass around this cleft and onto the Colsta headland, again staying close by the cliff edge as you continue on to Hoini and Kista.

> There are a lot of rocky skerries on the bay below the cliffs off these headlands, and you should have a look with binoculars to see whether there are any **seals** hauled out on the rocks.

Now the coast cuts in a little more to Hunds Heelor, and it is just a short walk around the bays of Reeva and Shirva to the final climb of the walk – the ascent up to Malcolm's Head.

The coastline swings away to the northwest, and the climb up to Malcolm's Head begins. The going is straightforward, and the views northwards along the west coast of the island that you've just traversed are memorable. Malcolm's Head summit is at 107m, and just offshore these is a narrow channel cutting off the stack of Fogli from the head itself.

Continue southwards downhill alongside the cliff edge. As you descend, keep an eye out for the big stone arches that grace this wonderful section of coastline. Seals can be seen basking on the skerries of the Crivv, then, as you descend further you come to a big rocky cleft at Mathers Head. Here there is a small jetty. Walk around the cleft and continue out to Head of Tind, a small rocky headland that is almost at sea level.

Just around the headland in South Harbour you reach the pier and the end of the public road that cuts across the island. Gain the road and head north, taking the right fork at the junction by the cemetery. Follow the lane past the Haa, and onwards to the school where the other lane is regained.

Turn right here, and follow the road northeastwards over the centre of the island and back to the pier in North Haven.

WALK 40

Mousa – the Mousa Broch and RSPB Reserve

Start/finish	At the pier at Leebotton (having booked a place on Tom Jamieson's boat Solan IV, tel 01950 431367, www.mousaboattrips.co.uk).
Grid ref	HU436248
Distance	2.8km/1.75 miles
Time	3 hours (between boats – check time of last boat back with Tom Jamieson)
Maps	OS Explorer 466; OS Landranger 4

During the Iron Age (600BC–500AD) many of the buildings erected in Scotland were defensible, round stone buildings known as brochs. They are double-walled, with the cavity between them having stairs leading to upper floors, as well as providing storage space. **Mousa Broch** is the best-preserved example in Scotland and rises to 12m (40 feet). You can still climb up to the highest level, making a walk to this broch a memorable experience.

Mousa is famous for its 2000-year-old broch. The walk itself is short, and suitable for those wanting to see the broch as well as those with an interest in wildlife.

The Mousa Broch

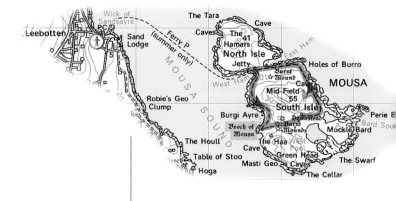

The trip over the Mousa Sound on Solan IV takes about half-an-hour, and there is a waymarked route around the central part of the island. The RSPB owns the island and asks that you stay on this path during the summer nesting season.

Mousa from Mainland

Once at the jetty on Mousa, follow the path round the bay of West Ham to the south. The route is obvious and you'll soon find yourself heading towards the broch. It's certainly an imposing sight, and you can have great fun scaling its tower.

During the summer months, Tom Jamieson runs special **night trips** to Mousa a couple of times each week. These need to be booked in advance, as they are very popular. Tom leaves at 23.00, returning at 00.30. The purpose of the trips is to allow you to be at the broch when the tiny storm petrels return to the island. The storm petrels nest in cavities in the broch walls, and spend the whole day out at sea, only returning to their nests at night. For many people this is the only chance they will ever have to see storm petrels.

From the broch head east over the centre of the island. There is a path that leads alongside a freshwater loch, passing to the north of the West Pool.

The West Pool is a great place to watch **common seals** on their pupping grounds. Stay well back from the pool, and move slowly and quietly so as not to disturb them. Seal pups have been known to get crushed by their parents if they are suddenly frightened – the adults make a mad dash for the water, flattening anything that gets in the way!

A little further along the path is the East Pool, another important seal-pupping ground. Here you'll also see Arctic terns on the nest, as well as eider ducks down by the shore.

The path now turns northwestwards, passing close to the east shore of the island. Follow it to the entrance to the large bay at East Ham, turning left along the south shore of this geo. From the head of East Ham there is a narrow neck of land running across the island. The path goes across this neck to the jetty at West Ham.

WALK 41
West Burra – Kettla Ness

Start/finish	Park sensibly at the end of the minor road south of Bridge End on the island of West Burra. This is reached via the island of Trondra, with causeways connecting the two islands to the Mainland near Scalloway.
Grid ref	HU368310
Distance	7.4km/4.6 miles
Time	3 hours
Maps	OS Explorer 466; OS Landranger 4

A short walk around the headland at the southern tip of West Burra.

Start at Duncansclett by continuing along the lane until it becomes a track. Here it passes over a narrow spit with the bay of Banna Minn to your right. Cross the spit on the path, then head northwards from Minn around the headland to Lotra of Minn.

The route follows the coast throughout and is a joy to walk. Look for otters around the bay at Clettnadal, and marvel at the impressive Fugla Stack. Arctic terns nest near the lake at Virda Vatn, and as you pass Spirls Geo, where there is a natural arch, you should see black guillemots and shags nesting on the cliffs below.

Towards the southern end of Kettla Ness there is an Ordnance Survey triangulation pillar marking the high point at 48m, and west of here is a superb peninsula jutting out to the northwest. This is known as the Heugg, and it is worth walking out right to the very tip.

Now follow the coast southwards around the wonderfully named Tinklee Geo, passing by a couple of skerries and another bay with some sea caves at its back. The next headland is Kettla Ness, and here the views south to the small islands of South Harva and Little Harva are stunning.

East Burra and the Clift Hills from West Burra

Continue around the coast to Groot Ness, where the short cliffs now lead you northeastwards into the mouth of West Voe. West Voe lies between Kettla Ness headland on West Burra and Houss Ness on East Burra, and is a great place to watch for seals.

The route now leads around the Bight of the Sandy Geos before bringing you out onto the Point of Guide, then leads you gently northwards back to the spit of land at Minn.

WALK 42

*East Burra – Houss Ness and the
Ward of Symbister*

Start/finish	Park sensibly at the end of the minor road on East Burra at Houss. East Burra is reached via the island of Trondra, with causeways connecting the two islands to Mainland near Scalloway.
Grid ref	HU377312
Distance	5.6km/3.5 miles
Time	2 hours
Maps	OS Explorer 466; OS Landranger 4

Another very pleasant walk around a headland, this time on East Burra, overlooking Kettla Ness across the West Voe.

From Houss there is a path leading south to the very narrow neck of land that connects Houss Ness to the rest of East Burra. Take the path across the neck and follow it around the west side of the Ness, beneath the hill of Ward of Symbister.

The path leads above the coast to a couple of old houses overlooking the channel of the Houb, but our way continues southwestwards along the coast. Pass Clivland Bay on the right and continue to the fabulously named Scaalie Point.

Look eastwards from Scaalie Point to a rugged line of cliffs running down to Point of Stakka, and here you'll see a spectacular natural arch. Just offshore, the teeth-like Stacks of Houssness add to the overall grandeur of the scene. Walk around the bay separating the two

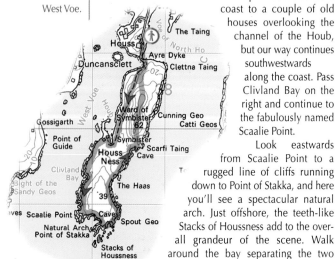

Puffin in flight

headlands, and gaze down to the rocks supporting the stacks and the Point of Stakka.

Now head north along the east coast of Houss Ness, passing by the skerry known as the Haas. Just beyond the Haas there is a little promontory jutting out into the water. This is known as Scarfi Taing, and it makes a great viewing point north and south along the deep channel of Clift Sound. Across Clift Sound to the east the Clift Hills rise dramatically to the summits of Royl Field, Holm Field and Muskna Field.

From Scarfi Taing you should leave the coast and head due north, climbing steeply for a short distance up to the summit of Ward of Symbister, 62m. The views from this lowly hill are surprisingly impressive, leading the eye along the length of Clift Sound to the east, while westwards, over Kettla Ness, the island of Foula can be seen far out in the North Atlantic.

Walk north from the summit cairn on Ward of Symbister, following a ridge down to the narrow neck of land, Ayre Dyke, that connects the Ness to East Burra. Pick up the path and follow it northwards back to Houss.

Walking around the Knab

MAINLAND CENTRAL

WALK 43
Lerwick Old Town and the Knab

Start/finish	There is a large pay-and-display car park on the pier in Lerwick, well signposted throughout the town.
Grid ref	HU477414
Distance	2.5km/1.5 miles
Time	1 hour
Maps	OS Explorer 466; OS Landranger 4

From the pier follow the road to the left, southwards onto Church Road. Follow Church Road up a hill to a mini roundabout. Here follow a road to the left – Annsbrae Place (*not* Knab Road). Continue down Clairmont Place and onto Scalloway Road. Now turn left onto St Olaf Street and soon find yourself looking out across the huge bay of Brei Wick.

Turn left along the road and look for a path on the right signposted for the Knab. Follow this path beneath the golf course. As you walk, stop to look over the low wall on the seaward side. Here there are grey seals basking on the rocks, while eider ducks and shags can be seen in large flotillas bobbing on the water. Also look for black guillemots nesting alongside fulmars on the cliffs.

Follow the path to a small car park (the end of Knab Road). Walk across this to the right and take the path signposted Twageos. This path passes above lovely little bays where turnstones, redshank and more eiders can be seen. Across the

A delightful short stroll around a fabulous headland, giving superb views all round, and introducing you to some of the wildlife that you will see elsewhere on Shetland.

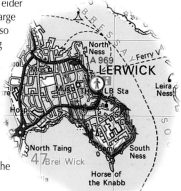

129

The Lodberry

Look for the old buildings of Lodberry on the right. These fishermen's cottages back right onto the sound, giving access to the water directly from the rear of the houses.

Bressay Sound you can see the large island of Bressay, with its impressive rocky headlands.

Follow the path until it becomes a road, and follow this on the right down Commercial Street. ◀

Continue along Commercial Street back into town. You'll find the pier on the right.

Beyond the pier and above Commercial Street is the superb viewpoint of Fort Charlotte.

Fort Charlotte

WALK 44

Scalloway to the Hill of Burwick

Start/finish	There is a car park overlooking the harbour in Scalloway.
Grid ref	HU404394
Distance	8.8km/5.5 miles
Time	4 hours
Maps	OS Explorer 466; OS Landranger 4

Walk along New Street in Scalloway, keeping the harbour to your left, then turn onto Main Street, going first to the museum.

From the summit of Hill of Burwick the view is of an amazing rock-studded seascape.

The museum has a fascinating display on **the 'Shetland Bus'**. During the Second World War, Norwegians sailed across the North Sea bringing refugees into Scalloway, often in the dead of night. They'd return with ammunition and saboteurs, risking their lives in German-patrolled waters for the sake of world peace.

Leave the museum and turn left, then left again along a street until you reach Berry Road on the right. Follow Berry Road to a farm, where you pick up a track climbing northwestwards around the eastern slopes of Hill of Berry. The track takes you up and over the north ridge of Hill of Berry, giving fine views back to Scalloway and its ruined castle.

Scalloway was once the capital of Shetland. The castle was built by forced labour in 1600. Patrick

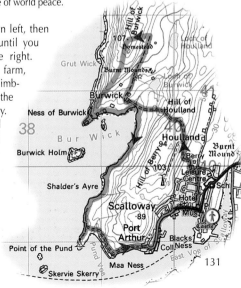

131

Scalloway in winter

Stewart had it built as his Shetland residence, and it is said that the mortar for holding the stones together was mixed with blood and eggs. Stewart was Earl of Orkney and Lord of Shetland, and half-brother to Mary Queen of Scots. He was executed in 1615, and in 1653 his castle at Scalloway became a temporary garrison for Cromwell's troops. Soon afterwards the castle became disused and fell into ruins.

Go over the crest of Hill of Berry, losing sight of Scalloway as you go. The track now drops steeply down the west side of the hill to where the stream issuing from the Loch of Burwick enters the sea at Bur Wick. Aim for this point, or head uphill slightly if you wish, to visit the Loch of Burwick itself.

At the stream, where you'll find the buildings of Burwick, you should cross to the west side and follow a path that heads northwards, climbing gently towards two burnt mounds. The path vanishes beyond these, and you head uphill to the summit of Hill of Burwick at 107m.

The **views to the west** take in a fabulous rock-studded seascape. Close by, the islands of Hildasay, Langa, Papa and Oxna dominate the view, while beyond, the coast of Westside stretches away into the distance, around Skelda Ness and on to Foula, way out in the North Atlantic.

You can return the same way to Scalloway, but I prefer to make this into a circuit by dropping down the southwest ridge from the summit of Hill of Burwick. This ridge narrows slightly as you descend, and you soon find yourself on the wonderful little headland of Ness of Burwick. Turn left and follow the coast to the farm at Burwick, re-crossing the stream you passed earlier.

Turn southwards along the coast, finding somewhat rough going at first, until you near the Point of Pund, with its little lighthouse set out on the promontory. Here you pick up a track that comes from the west end of Scalloway.

Follow the track eastwards, passing Maa Ness overlooking Pund Voe, and you soon enter Scalloway next to the North Atlantic Fisheries College. ▶

The restaurant at the North Atlantic Fisheries College is one of the best places to find fresh seafood anywhere in Britain.

WALK 45

Fora Ness

Start/finish	At Sand, parking sensibly by the telephone box.
Grid ref	HU343477
Distance	7.7km 4.8 miles
Time:	3 hours
Maps	OS Explorer 467; OS Landrangers 3 and 4

Start by walking east along the road from the telephone box. The lane passes between some old croft lands and is a good introduction to the area. At a junction by a cattle-grid you go straight ahead to Innersand, veering off left as you approach the farm buildings. There is a track here, and it leads east to a track junction. Turn right and head south to the old buildings at Foraness.

South lies the wonderful narrow Fora Ness peninsula. You can walk anywhere you like down here, favouring the higher ground along the spine of the peninsula if you prefer, but I like to work my way around the coast, going anti-clockwise.

A walk that explores the lovely Fora Ness peninsula.

The going is easy at first, then, as you come onto slightly steeper ground, a little harder to walk, with rough terrain underfoot. However, it is never too difficult, and the views westwards across Sand Voe are lovely.

At Seli Geo the way gets a little rockier, and you can walk out to a number of little headlands between Seli Geo, Blo Geo, and as you round the corner to the east, Red Geo. Off the southern tip of Fora Ness, just east of Blo Geo, is the little island of Fore Holm. Beyond lie the scattered Lunga Skerries. ◄

I recently asked a sailor what the difference is between a skerry and an island. His reply was that an island is big enough to graze a sheep!

Once on the east side of the peninsula, north of Red Geo, is a big bay at Brei Geo, and here you can often see seals in the water. Continue northwards along the eastern side of Fora Ness, and as you approach the narrow channel known as Sandsound Voe, you should head west to pick up the track just south of Innersand. Return northwards along the track and then the road to your car.

WALK 46

Easter Skeld to Skelda Ness

Start/finish	Park in Easter Skeld by the road junction.
Grid ref	HU310449
Distance	13.7km/8.5 miles
Time	4–5 hours
Maps	OS Explorer 467; OS Landranger 4

Head off down the little lane to the southwest, soon leaving the houses of East Skeld behind, and passing the school on your right. Look out for the Loch of Arg away to your right – this is a good place to spot red-throated divers.

Beyond the Loch of Arg you reach a road junction. Turn left here and head south along the lane for Scarvister. Continue right to the end of the road, then where it continues southwards as a track, take this up to the Loch of Scarvister – another good place for red-throated divers, and here you might also see a few curlew too.

Continue along the track to the south, making a slight detour up to the top of the hill on the right to visit the prominent OS trig pillar on Shoostran if you wish. Soon the path fizzles out as you approach the end of Skelda Ness, but the going here is straightforward.

It's worth continuing right to the tip of the peninsula to see the wonderful setting of Moulie Loch, which lies just back from the cliff edge above the rocky defile of East Moulie Geo.

Walk out to the very tip of the Skelda Ness peninsula, a little rocky bluff known as Spoothellier, then double back to continue westwards to West Moulie Geo.

This lovely route along a peninsula includes a little road walking, but the lanes are never busy, and the easy terrain allows you to stride out and enjoy big skies and wonderful views.

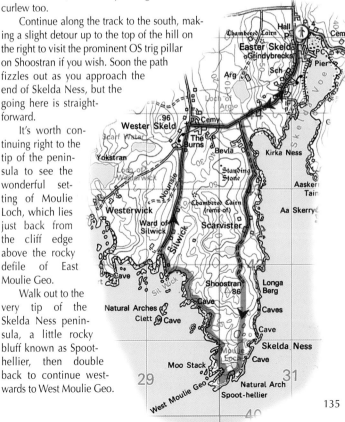

135

Look for nesting fulmars here, as well as shags, black guillemots and rock doves.

Now follow the coast northwestwards, marvelling at the wonderful rock architecture of the stack out in the bay. Clett has a fabulous natural arch, and from a cairn above Squidel you can look across to the pinnacles of rock that form Berga Stack and Erne's Stack.

As you approach Berga Stack you'll start to see a few houses over on the right. This is the hamlet of Silwick, and a track comes down to the cliff edge from the southern end of a dead-end road. Follow this track northwards to meet the road, and continue along the lane to the village of Wester Skeld.

As you come in to the village, ignore the lane leading off to the left, and continue to a road junction by a chapel. Turn right here, passing a telephone box on the right and continuing to the junction near Loch of Arg that you passed earlier. Turn left at this junction and retrace your steps northeastwards, back to Easter Skeld.

The Scord of Brouster (Walk 47)

WALK 47

The Scord of Brouster

Start/finish	Park on the side of the A971, by a sign pointing to the Scord of Brouster – this is just west of Bridge of Walls.
Grid ref	HU255514
Distance	0.4km/0.2 miles
Time	Half an hour
Maps	OS Explorer 467; OS Landranger 3

A short stroll in a wonderful part of Walls to a remarkable archaeological site. Definitely one for the prehistory buff, and those with a passing interest should also find it interesting.

The walk itself needs no description. The site is almost on the side of the A971, and is waymarked from the parking place.

The **Scord of Brouster** is an open hillside littered with the remains of what was once an extensive Neolithic settlement – oval houses and interlinking field systems can be seen. The whole site dates from about 2000BC, and there is also a perfectly circular kerbed cairn, and a large oblong stone enclosure, all from the same period.

Walking at the Scord of Brouster

WALK 48

Staneydale Temple

Start/finish	Park on the side of the minor road running south from the A971, by a sign pointing to the Staneydale Temple; this is overlooking the Loch of Gruting.
Grid ref	HU292502
Distance	2.4km/1.5 miles
Time	1 hour
Maps	OS Explorer 467; OS Landranger 3

A walk similar to the Scord of Brouster – indeed, the two sites are often visited one after the other as they are close together.

The walk is straightforward, and follows a good path all the way across open moorland to the 'temple'. Look out for the cairns and the group of Neolithic houses alongside the path.

Staneydale Temple is actually a wonderful Neolithic site dating back to around 3000BC. The main feature on the site is an oval structure with a single entrance

Inside Staneydale Temple

passage leading into the large hall. There are half-a-dozen alcoves leading off the main hall, each separated by huge stone pillars, and it is thought that such a substantial building was probably the chieftain's house. It almost certainly wasn't a 'temple'.

Walk back the same way.

WALK 49

Mu Ness to Deepdale over Sandness Hill

Start/finish	Park at Dale of Walls.
Grid ref	HU180525
Distance	13.2km /8.2 miles
Time	5 hours
Maps	OS Explorer 467, OS Landranger 3
Note	Map and compass skills required.

Start by walking along the lane northwestwards towards the farms at Netherdale, turning left just before the telephone box. Climb uphill to a gate that leads out onto the open fell and continue northwards onto the broad ridge of Blouk Field. Now turn to the northeast and follow the ridge to the top of this minor hill.

Descend to the north and climb gently up the other side of a broad col, gaining the summit of Dale Hill at a cairn at 184m.

To the north is the steep-sided valley of Deep Dale, with the large bulk of Sandness Hill on its north side. The summit of Sandness Hill is your next destination, but rather than making straight for it, the best route is to follow the broad connecting ridge between Dale Hill and Sandness Hill. This runs to the northeast, and you can follow it for a mile until the summit of Sandness Hill lies above you to the north.

This wild walk over some of the more remote hills of Mainland is never very difficult, but in some places you feel a long way from anywhere, which is one of its many attractions.

139

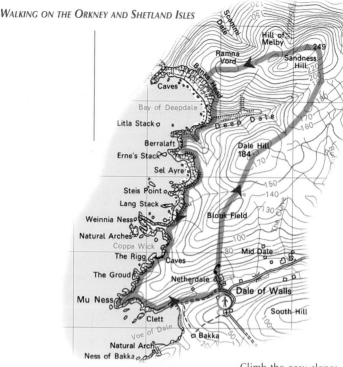

Climb the easy slopes to the top at 249m. The summit is marked by an ancient cairn and an Ordnance Survey triangulation pillar. The views from Sandness Hill are far-reaching. They stretch northwards to the lovely little island of Papa Stour, and westwards towards distant Foula.

The western flank of Sandness Hill is interesting. There is a tarn, known as Nether Shun, high up just beneath the summit ridge, and two ridges fall away from the flat area where this tarn sits. To the north is a rounded spur known as Hill of Melby, while to the west lies the cairned ridge of Ramna Vord.

From Sandness Hill you should head west to Nether Shun, then continue just south of west along the superb ridge of Ramna Vord, the island of Foula seeming to float in the distance ahead of you.

Deepdale from Ramna Vord

From the cairn on Ramna Vord drop down to the southwest to the magnificent sweep of broken ground and scree-covered cliffs that is Banks Head. This flank of Ramna Vord falls directly into the sea at Bay of Deepdale, 150m (490 feet) below.

Turn southwards along the cliff edge and descend into the trough of Deep Dale. If you keep close to the cliffs you'll get a spectacular view of the waterfall where the Burn of Deepdale plunges off the cliff, falling 60m (195 feet) into the bay below.

Cross the stream carefully – picking a safe spot well back from the cliff edge. Once on the south side follow the magnificent serrated coastline around, wandering out to the narrow arête overlooking Erne's Stack to the southwest of Deep Dale.

Old Norse kiln below Sandness Hill with Papa Stour beyond

Continue around the cliff tops, around the bay of Sel Ayre, and then onwards to a huge, almost-detached fang of rock known as Weinnia Ness. You can scramble out to the grassy top of this and admire the amazing views down both sides.

Back on the cliff top continue southwards around the wild voe of Coppa Wick, walking out to the south-west to the headland of Mu Ness. There is a promontory at the extreme end of the headland, and you can walk out onto this to get fine views of the rock stacks of Buid Stacks and Clett, and over a narrow channel to the bulging rock of Skerry of Dale.

The old pier at Noonsbrough (Walk 50)

Now head eastwards along the coast, around the north shore of Voe of Dale. You'll come to a track that heads inland alongside a stream, and if you follow this eastwards you'll soon find yourself back at Netherdale, then on to Dale of Walls.

WALK 50
Ness of Noonsbrough

Start/finish	Park sensibly near the road junction overlooking the Voe of Setter.
Grid ref	HU303566
Distance	6.9km/4.3 miles
Time	3 hours
Maps	OS Explorer 467; OS Landranger 3

Begin by strolling along the lane to the northwest, making for the hamlet of Noonsbrough. As you walk, keep an eye out for a pile of white wooden stanchions lying on the grass. These are the remains of the old pier at

Another beautiful walk around a remote peninsula, initially along a minor road to an ancient broch overlooking Voe of Clousta, then along the peninsula's wild and rough central belt.

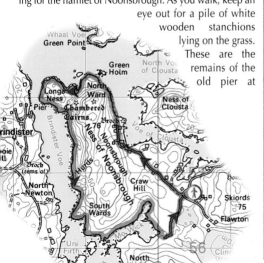

Noonsbrough, and the white covering is actually thousands of tiny barnacles, not paint!

Continue walking to the end of the road, then, as you approach the houses in the tiny boatyard, go down to the waterside on the right. There is a ruinous broch here which you can have a look at before continuing.

Walk along the shore from the broch until you are clear of the fenced area, then climb diagonally up the hill. Aim northwestwards and you soon reach the top of the hill known as Dutch Ward. There is an ancient cairn up here at 76m above sea level.

> **Dutch Ward** is un-named on the Landranger map, but named on the Explorer. Just to the north of the summit cairn, 275m (300 yards) away, there is another rise, and this is known as North Ward, marked as such on both maps. The views northwards from these little hills are spectacular. Just across the water is the island of Vementry, while Muckle Roe lies beyond.

Head north from Dutch Ward to North Ward, then descend down the north face to the sea. Walk around the coastline to the west, crossing over the flatter area of Longa Ness, overlooking the sea channel of Brindister Voe.

Head southwards now, along the east shore of Brindister Voe. There is some rough ground to cross here – mainly thick bracken and moorland grasses interspersed with clumps of heather.

On your right the channel of Brindister Voe narrows at the entrance to Uni Firth. Continue around the coast here, heading eastwards where another channel cuts in. This channel is Mo Wick, and is a great place to look for otters.

Follow the north side of Mo Wick to its head, then walk eastwards across boggy ground to gain a track. This track goes northeastwards and will return you to the road junction near which you parked.

The view from the Ness of Noonsbrough

WALK 51

Scalla Field and the Butter Stone

Start/finish	There is a designated car park by a sign for the Burn of Lunklet, on the B9071 between Voe and Aith.
Grid ref	HU367576
Distance	9km/5.6 miles
Time	3 hours
Maps	OS Explorer 467; OS Landranger 2 or 3
Note	Map and compass skills required.

This hill walk takes you through some remote and little-visited country, to the summits of two of the higher hills of central Mainland.

On the north side of the Burn of Lunklet, where a road bridge crosses the burn on a big bend, just before the burn flows into the sea at East Burra Firth, there is a signpost pointing along a laid footpath. There is a duckboard here, and the sign points to the Burn of Lunklet.

Follow the path alongside the burn to a lovely little waterfall. Now continue, still on the north side of the burn, to a point where three streams all come down to the same place. From the north, the Burn of Marrofield-water drains the boggy ground in that

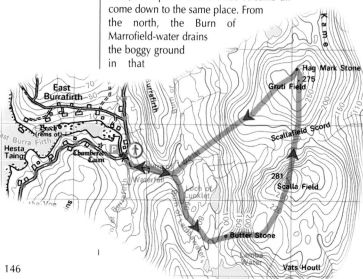

The start of the path up Scalla Field

direction, while from the south the Burn of Lambawater flows from the picturesque tarn of Lamba Water. The Burn of Lunklet splashes down from the Loch of Lunklet to the east.

Cross to the east side of the Burn of Lambawater and follow it southwards, climbing gradually uphill. As the gradient begins to level out you get a sudden view of Lamba Water, and if you're lucky you might also see red-throated divers fishing on the loch, or perhaps feeding young here.

Don't walk as far as the shores of Lamba Water, but instead climb up the hill to the east, aiming for the Butter Stone. This is a great place to sit and admire the splendid views.

From the **Butter Stone** the views are dominated by the rugged and ragged coastline. It can be difficult at times to make out which bits of land belong to Mainland and which bits are islands. However, with a map to hand you should be able to spot the islands of Vementry, Papa Little, Muckle Roe, and away to the right, beyond the short voe of Gon Firth, the small islet of Linga.

Nearer at hand to the northwest is the lovely little tarn of Loch of Lunklet. You should scan the waters here for red-throated divers, and you might see common sandpipers here during the summer too.

The Lunklet Burn

Above the Butter Stone the hillside is quite steep. However, if you climb up eastwards you soon come out onto a flatter area. The summit of Scalla Field lies just over half a mile to the northeast from here. Cross the moorland and climb the easy slopes to the summit. This is marked by a trig pillar, and at 281m is something of a high point for this part of the island.

North of Scalla Field the ground drops away to a col, known as Scallafield Scord. Drop down into this, aiming slightly to the northeast from the summit of the hill. Once at the high point of the col, aim slightly northwest, climbing again, and you'll soon top out on Gruti Field, another low hill at 275m.

Now turn to the southwest, descending gently along a very broad ridge. You'll get a view southwards of the Loch of Lunklet, and if you aim just to the right of this as you drop down, you'll reach the Burn of Lunklet where it sploshes down the hill. Turn downhill and follow this burn on its north side all the way back to the road.

WALK 52

The North Nesting Coast

Start/finish	Park at the top of the hill at Kirk Ward, on the B9075 between Laxo and Brettabister.
Grid ref	HU472583
Distance	12.8km /8 miles
Time	4–5 hours
Maps	OS Explorers 467 and 468; OS Landranger 2 or 3

From the top of Kirk Ward hill begin the walk by following the road southeastwards down to Brettabister. Near the bottom of the hill there's a road junction by a memorial and you should turn left here, following the lane towards Housabister and Kirkabister.

As you walk toward Housabister, look out for the remains of a broch on the right, just before you reach the chapel at Housabister.

Walk on through Housabister and Kirkabister until you reach the road end at Neap. Go through the yard at the farm, and just to the left of the buildings here there is a track that leads in a big curve to the southwest, then back to the

This walk takes you along the spine of North Nesting headland, on the east coast of Mainland, south of Dury Voe, after traversing the spectacular coastline.

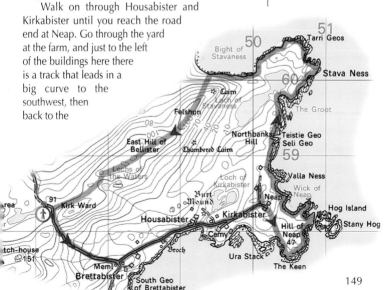

east. Follow this track until you are clear of Neap and can wander freely about the open Hill of Neap.

Head south, down to the coast at the Keen.

The delightful walk around the coast leads initially eastwards, passing above the rough coastline at Dringa Neap, then along narrow Hog Sound. The sound separates Mainland from the little islets of Hog Island and Stany Hog. ◄

> Hog Island has the remains of an Iron Age fort on its west side, overlooking the sound.

Continue northwards along the coast, passing a large bay and another small headland before walking along the top of Wick of Neap.

The route continues around the shore, keeping above the cliffs of Doves Cove and Valla Ness, and then onwards to the dramatic in-cut gloups of Seli Geo and Teistie Geo. Walk on, northwards, to a fantastic gully known as the Groot. Here there is a lake, the Loch of Stavaness, set just back from the shore, and the Groot is the spot where this loch drains into the sea.

Cross to the northeast side of the Groot and continue around the coast to Stava Ness.

The coastal section of this walk is nearly over, so enjoy the walk around from Stava Ness to Tarri Geos. To the west of Tarri Geos a big bay, the Bight of Stavaness, opens out, and you walk around the bay until the moorland ridge on the left comes down to meet the coast.

Climb the ridge, gaining good views over the Loch of Stavaness, and stop to enjoy views over the eastern islands from the ancient cairn known as Stany Cuml. Above Stany Cuml the ridge becomes more pronounced, and you follow it southwestwards over Fleshun and on to East Hill of Bellister.

> Keep an eye out for **mountain hares** on this rough moorland hill. There are a number of sites in the Shetlands that are good for these wild creatures, and this is one of the best!

Continue southwestwards from the summit of East Hill of Bellister, passing just above the Lochs of the Waters, and you soon reach your car parked at the top of Kirk Ward.

CENTRAL ISLANDS

WALK 53

Foula – the Daal to the Sneck Ida Smallie

Start/finish	At the pier in Ham Voe, at the eastern side of the island of Foula.
Grid ref	HT974387
Distance	8.3km /5.2 miles
Time	3 hours
Maps	OS Explorer 467; OS Landranger 4

Walk along the lane from the pier, going north then west through the village, which is rather grandly named the Toon o' Ham. Climb slightly uphill, then, as you approach a cottage on the left, look for a path, also on the left, that takes you down to cross the head of the little channel of the Voe.

Follow this path and climb up the other side of the channel to gain the end of a minor road. Walk southwestwards along this lane, passing a mast, until you reach a junction. Turn left here and continue along the lane, passing the island's tiny chapel on the right and the landing strip on the left.

Just beyond the chapel you'll see a path on the right heading towards an obvious valley, the

A fine moorland walk on one of the most remote inhabited islands of Britain. If you have time between boats, continue over the Noup (see Walk 55), otherwise the walk out to the Sneck Ida Smallie is superb.

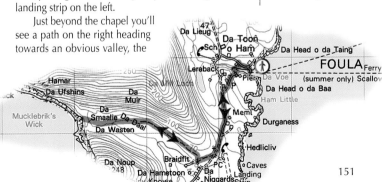

151

The Sneck Ida Smallie

Daal. Walk westwards initially, then northwestwards on the path up the Daal, avoiding being bonked by bonxies as you go.

> Bonxies are also known as **great skuas**. They are huge piratical birds of the sea, and they make their living from attacking other seabirds until the victim is forced to vomit its last meal. The bonxies then tuck in! If you approach them on their nesting grounds you should be aware that they are not above dive-bombing walkers too!

The path up the Daal is dull initially, save for the ever-present bonxies. However, as you near the western end of the dale, where the ground flattens before plunging from the steep cliffs on the western side of the island, you should veer slightly to the northwest, to reach a massive cleft in the rock face. This is the top edge of the Sneck Ida Smallie, a narrow, rocky gully, green with algae and moss. ◄

Local legend has it that this is where the small people, or trolls, brew up bad weather, as well as trouble!

Return the same way.

WALK 54

Foula – the Sneug

Start/finish	At the pier in Ham Voe, at the eastern side of the island of Foula.
Grid ref	HT974387
Distance	5km/8 miles
Time	3 hours
Maps	OS Explorer 467; OS Landranger 4
Note	Map and compass skills required.

Walk along the lane from pier, continuing westwards to where it is joined by another lane that runs from the southern end of the island to the northern hamlet of the Nort Toons.

Turn to the right at this junction and follow the lane above the Crookit Burn for just over a mile, until the lane turns sharply to the right. Ignore this turn to the right, and instead go straight ahead on a track, soon gaining the open hillside by a cairn.

Now climb steadily to the north of Blobers Burn, heading westwards along a ridge known as Soberlie. Follow this ridge until you get to the edge of the fantastic cliffs on the northwest coast of the island. Now turn to

A superb mountain ascent to the highest hill on the island of Foula.

Mill Loch below the Sneug on Foula

The sea cliffs falling from the Kame are among the highest in Britain, dropping for 375m (1230ft) straight into the broiling waters below.

the southwest and climb upwards, very gently at first along the Nort Bank, then with increasing steepness as you tackle the final summit cone of the Kame. ◄

The summit of the Kame is a magical place, offering wild views along the northwest and southwest coasts of this remarkably remote island. To the southeast rises the highest point of the island, the Sneug, and a fine connecting ridge leads to its top.

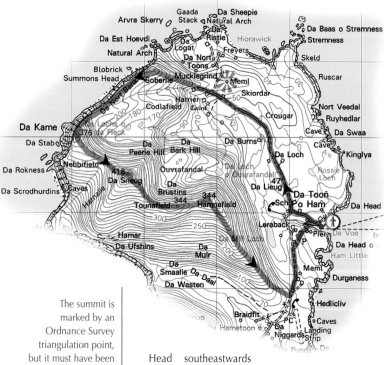

The summit is marked by an Ordnance Survey triangulation point, but it must have been a rare day for the surveyors to be able to spot two others pillars from here.

Head southeastwards from the Kame, dropping to a col with a number of little pools just above the lowest part. From the col just beyond climb gently up to the summit of the Sneug, a superb viewpoint at 418m. ◄

Now descend to the southeast, curving along a ridge to the east. This ridge is known as Hamnafield, and towards its eastern end the ground drops away very suddenly. Here you're overlooking the Toon o' Ham way below, but the direct route down is very steep indeed. This flank of the hill is known as the Wavy Stanes, and is best avoided. Instead, follow the ridge to the southeast, known as Bodlifield. This takes you downhill for over a mile to join a minor road near to the island's tiny chapel.

Turn left along this road until you reach a junction. Now take the lane to the right, dropping slightly to the head of the Voe. A path leads down to the head of the small natural harbour, and from there you climb up to a cottage just above the pier. Turn right along a lane, reached at the cottage, and you'll be at the pier in minutes.

WALK 55
Foula – the Noup

Start/finish	At the pier in Ham Voe, at the eastern side of the island of Foula.
Grid ref	HT974387
Distance	8.8km /5.5 miles
Time	3–4 hours
Maps	OS Explorer 467; OS Landranger 4

Walk along the lane from the pier, going north then west through the village. Climb slightly uphill, then, as you approach a cottage on the left, look for a path, also on the left, that takes you down to cross the head of the little channel of the Voe. Follow this and climb up the other side to gain the end of a minor road.

Walk southwestwards along this lane, passing a mast, until you reach a junction. Turn left here and walk along the lane. Go past the chapel on the right and the landing strip on the left. Just beyond the chapel you'll see a path on the right heading up the Daal. Walk westwards

An excursion via the Sneck Ida Smallie to the marvellous cone of the Noup.

Walking on the Noup on Foula

initially, then northwestwards on the path up the Daal, to reach the Sneck Ida Smallie (as for Walk 53).

After enjoying the spectacular views down the Sneck Ida Smallie, return to the south, climbing up the

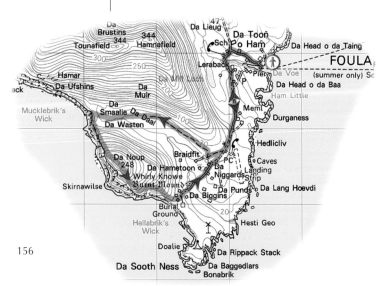

magnificent cone of the Noup. The going is easy, over short-cropped grass, and the summit is soon reached at 248m. The cliffs to the southwest fall away straight into the crashing waves that pile in from the North Atlantic, while fulmars, kittiwakes and rock doves nest on the ledges below.

Follow the grassy hillside to the southeast, then eastwards down to the road end at the scattered hamlet of Hametoun. Turn northeastwards along the road and follow it back past the chapel, then retrace your outward route back to the pier.

WALK 56

Bressay – the Ward of Bressay and the Ord

Start/finish	At the pier where the ferry from Lerwick drops you off.
Grid ref	HU487417
Distance	15km/9.4 miles
Time	5–6 hours
Maps	OS Explorer 466; OS Landranger 4

Start the walk by following the road around the little harbour, then eastwards up the hill to a junction. Turn right here, then bear right again almost immediately. You should now be following the lane on the east shore of the Voe of Leiraness towards the little lighthouse and school.

At the chapel turn left, walking eastwards to a crossroads by the school. Take a right along the lane, then a left where this bends around to the right. Walk southeastwards to another bend in the road, and just before this look for a footpath on the left that climbs steadily uphill to the east. Take this path, reaching another little public road by a few scattered houses.

Go left to a junction, then right immediately, looking for the continuation of the path, now heading to the southeast. This path takes to the open hill, taking you up

The island of Bressay lies just east from Lerwick, across the Bressay Sound, and is easy to reach as a foot passenger on board one of the regular ferries.

The Ward of Bressay

a ridge to the minor top of West Hill at 150m.

Descend to the south into a col, then veer southwest, climbing gently and crossing a couple of tracks that cut across the slopes. Aim for the obvious masts on the summit of Ward of Bressay and you'll soon be at the top of the highest summit of Bressay, at 226m. Follow the south ridge for half a mile, then curve away to the southwest to a tarn high on the Black Hill. Continue walking to the south-west, keeping to the high ground along this vague ridge, until you come up against the steep sea cliffs of the Ord. Keep the cliffs to

Bressay from Noss

your left and walk northwestwards now, descending to the superbly situated Kirkabister lighthouse.

From the lighthouse follow the access lane northwards, passing the farms at Kirkabister, then continuing to a road junction by a telephone box at Grindiscol. Here go straight ahead, northwards along the lane through Glebe, then on to the crossroads by the school, which you crossed earlier in the day.

Retrace your steps back to the pier, in time for the ferry back to Lerwick.

WALK 57

Noss – the Noss Head Nature Reserve

Start/finish	At the pier on the island of Noss, where the little passenger ferry (summer only) crosses the Noss Sound from the east side of Bressay.
Grid ref	HU530410
Distance	10km/6.3 miles
Time	3–4 hours
Maps	OS Explorer 466; OS Landranger 4
Note	The ferry to Noss from Bressay is inflatable. Dogs are not allowed.

The island of Noss is a superb place to immerse yourself in the wildlife of these shores. This walk takes you on a clockwise tour of the coast of the island.

Follow the north coast up North Croo from the landing place, then turn south above the Cletters and climb steeply to Noss Head, where thousands of seabirds clamour all around.

During the **summer breeding season** around 45,000 guillemots, 7000 pairs of gannets and several thousand fulmars, kittiwakes and puffins noisily crowd ledges beneath Noss Head. Also, keep a look

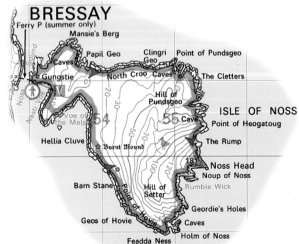

Razorbills on Noss

out for seals in the surrounding seas, and piratical bonxies on the moorland of the interior.

From Noss Head continue around the coast, descending to Noup of Noss, then skirting around Rumble Wick bay. The coast then falls along Hill of Setter as you descend to Holm of Noss and Feadda Ness.

Here the coast takes you to the northwest, along Point of Hovie, to Voe of Mells. There's a small headland jutting out to the south along the western shore of the Voe, and just over this is the landing place where the inflatable ferry will pick you up for the return to Bressay.

WALK 58
Papa Stour – Virda Field and Mauns Hill

Start/finish	At the pier in Housa Voe, on the big eastern bay of Papa Stour.
Grid ref	HU183608
Distance	11.5km /7.2 miles
Time	4–5 hours
Maps	OS Explorer 467; OS Landranger 3

Some of the most impressive coastline in Shetland is found on Papa Stour, including caves, arches, stacks and skerries. This walk takes you over to the wild west coast, via paths leading easily across this rugged island.

Start by heading west from the pier, passing Gardie as you bend around on the island's only road, making for Biggings to the south. At the bend to the south there is a track that leads west. Follow this for just over a quarter of a mile, until it bends to the north.

Don't follow the track around the bend, but instead continue northwestwards on a path that leads around to the northern end of Gorda Water. The path is superb, and takes you westwards to an old homestead, then south-westwards to a junction of paths overlooking Dutch Loch.

Turn right at the path junction, climbing gently as you ascend a broad ridge to Little Virda Field. The path continues to the northwest to the summit of Virda Field, at 87m the high point of the island, and marked by an OS trig pillar.

From the top of Virda Field drop down to the south-west, to a big gulf in the cliffs known as Akers Geo. Skirt around this cleft to its south side, and follow the coast-line around the Horn to Hund Geo.

Now the way follows the coast, passing some won-derful rock scenery as you make your way southeast-wards to Wilma Skerry. There are a number of natural arches to look for in the cliff bases, and lots of seabirds wheeling around too.

From Wilma Skerry, a rocky outcrop overlooking the western limits of Hamna Voe, you should stay with the coast as it bend to the northeast. The way keeps close by

the western side of Hamna Voe, and it is possible to detour slightly to the left to gain Mauns Hills.

Papa Stour

At the head of Hamna Voe is a stream that runs from Dutch Loch to the voe itself. Cross this and pick up a path to the

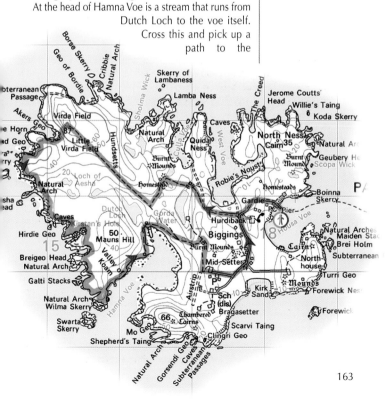

southeast, keeping to it as it curves to the south towards the airstrip. Now walk eastwards out onto the narrow lane, and follow it northwards to return to the pier in Housa Voe.

WALK 59

Whalsay – the Ward of Clett

Start/finish	At the pier in Symbister, on Whalsay.
Grid ref	HU536623
Distance	3.9km/2.4 miles
Time	2 hours
Maps	OS Explorer 468; OS Landranger 2

This walk is a short stroll to the highest point of the island, the Ward of Clett.

The island of Whalsay is a real haven. Lots of fishing boats, large and small, crowd the harbour at Symbister, and colourful houses stand along the water's edge. After exploring Symbister itself, head east, away from the harbour area.

Take the lane leading south towards Harlsdale and Sandwick, continuing south at the road junction in Sandwick. The lane now bends to the right before bringing you in a big sweep back to the southeast, ending at the tiny hamlet of Clate. From Clate you can follow a track to the southeast, up to a quarry, then follow it uphill as it zigzags up the southwestern ridge of the Ward of Clett. The top is soon reached at 119m, and is marked by an OS trig pillar.

Return via the same route.

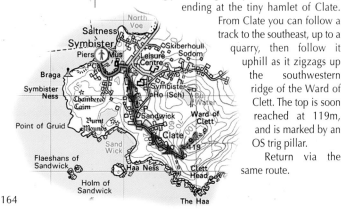

164

WALK 60

Out Skerries – Housay and Mio Ness

Start/finish	At the pier at Bruray, overlooking South Mouth on the remote island of Out Skerries.
Grid ref	HU688716
Distance	8km/5 miles
Time	3–4 hours
Maps	OS Explorer 468; OS Landranger 2

Start by following the lane to the northwest, passing the island's airstrip and the fire station. Continue west down to the Skerries Bridge, which connects the two separate islands of Bruray and Housay. Cross the bridge and continue along the lane, ignoring the junction where another leads off to the left.

Soon you reach another junction, with one lane going straight on for the chapel, and the other taking you right to the cemetery. Take this latter lane northwards for a short way. The lane soon becomes a track and

The wonderful islands of Out Skerries are a haven for lovers of peace, solitude and wildlife. This walk takes in the magical Housay, leading you to Mio Ness at its south-western tip.

curves around to the west coast at a jetty overlooking West Voe.

Shetland pony on the Out Skerries

Now the track ends and you must follow the coast, heading along the south side of West Voe towards Queyin Ness, a wild headland overlooking the narrow entrance to West Voe. Walk around Queyin Ness and into the bay of Cobbi Geo, then onwards again to the south-west, keeping the shore close by all the while.

Beyond the next little headland, the Steig, there is a narrow neck of land connecting Housay to the Ward of Mioness. Cross this neck via rocky ground, and continue down the western coast of the island until you reach Mio Ness, the southwesterly tip of Housay. From Mio Ness you can see the whole of Whalsay and Mainland spread out on the western horizon. Immediately to the south are the islets of North Benelip and South Benelip, while the Easter Skerries are hidden from view behind them.

Turn the corner of Mio Ness and begin walking back along the other side of the peninsula, heading northeastwards with the open sea out to your right. You soon find yourself at the other end of the narrow neck of land connecting you back to the rest of Housay, and here there are some wonderful pools on your right, in a bay known as Trolli Geo.

Continue around the south coast of Housay, sticking close by the shore, or moving further inland as the fancy takes you. As you near the southeastern end of Housay you come up against South Mouth, the channel that cuts between Housay and Bruray, and here you'll be forced to head northwest, picking up the end of a lane.

Follow the lane past the post office to a junction. If you now turn right you'll be retracing your steps down and over Skerries Bridge, and so back to the pier on Bruray.

MAINLAND NORTH

WALK 61
Lunna Ness

Start/finish	At Lunna Kirk.
Grid ref	HU486691
Distance	18km/11.2 miles
Time	5–6 hours
Maps	OS Explorer 468; OS Landranger 2 or 3

Lunna Kirk was built in 1753. One of its interesting features is leper squint holes, where those who were afflicted could listen to the service from outside.

This is a lovely coastal walk around the peninsula of Lunna Ness.

Start at Lunna Kirk and walk southeastwards to the shore at East Lunna Voe. Walk along the shore of the voe, bearing northeastwards, with the sea lapping gently to your right. The route continues through the impressive fulmar colonies at Taing of Kelswick and Ramna Geo, then takes you onwards to Mill Loch and the narrow gully at Grut Wick.

Stick with the coast as you continue northeastwards, and you soon climb over a small knoll before descending to cross the stream issuing from the Loch of Stofast. Climb up the other side, still with the coast close by on your right, then cross another stream, this one coming from large Fulga Water. ▶

There are lots of small islets in Fugla Water, and many of these support colonies of nesting Arctic terns.

A little further along the coast you have the option of making a very slight detour to climb the Ward of Outrabister, at 90m the highest point on Lunna Ness. There is an OS trig pillar on the summit.

Return to the coast and continue around to the rocky headland of Stour Hedva. From here there are superb views out to Swarta Skerry, Longa Skerry, Lunna Holm and Sand Skerry, while further out you can see Whalsay and the Out Skerries.

Walk around the wild bay of Wick of Glachon and continue to the very end of the peninsula, Land Taing. The route now turns to the southwest, continuing

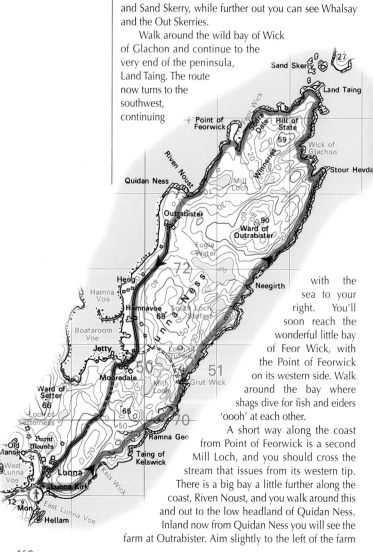

with the sea to your right. You'll soon reach the wonderful little bay of Feor Wick, with the Point of Feorwick on its western side. Walk around the bay where shags dive for fish and eiders 'oooh' at each other.

A short way along the coast from Point of Feorwick is a second Mill Loch, and you should cross the stream that issues from its western tip. There is a big bay a little further along the coast, Riven Noust, and you walk around this and out to the low headland of Quidan Ness. Inland now from Quidan Ness you will see the farm at Outrabister. Aim slightly to the left of the farm buildings and you hit a track. Turn right along this and follow it to the farm itself.

At the farm the track becomes a metalled road. Follow this southwestwards back to Lunna Kirk, passing a number of cottages and farms overlooking the huge gulf of Boatsroom Voe.

WALK 62

Ness of Hillswick

Start/finish	By the public toilets in the village of Hillswick.
Grid ref	HU282770
Distance	7.2km /4.5 miles
Time	2–3 hours
Maps	OS Explorer 469; OS Landranger 3

Walk south along the lane leading to Findlins House, then make your way down to the shore.

A popular walk around the rough peninsula just south of the village of Hillswick. Surprisingly, it is pathless for much of the way, and there are a few fences to cross.

This is a great place to see **otters**. Coastal otters prefer to come out hunting on a rising tide, and so are not necessarily nocturnal, as many people believe. We only have one species of otter in Britain, the Eurasian otter, Lutra lutra. On the rivers of England and Wales this species is pretty much completely nocturnal, but by the coast in Scotland it can be seen at any time of day.

Continue around the little headland of Tur Ness that juts out into Ura Firth, then on into the bay known as the Bight of Niddister.

Watch for **fulmars** as you walk along towards Baa Taing. These graceful birds are a joy to watch as they skim close to the waves out at sea. They look not unlike seagulls, but are in fact members of the shearwater family. They fly with very stiff wings, whereas gulls are much more flappy.

Continue around the Quilse and into Queen Geos, then on to the lighthouse at Baa Taing, the headland of the Ness of Hillswick.

From Baa Taing turn northwestwards and continue along the coast, passing the finger-like pinnacle of Gordi Stack, and Windy Geo, before climbing to the 70m cliff top of Oris Field. Out to sea across Houlma Sound you can see the famous rock pinnacles of the Isle of Westerhouse and the Drongs.

Continue around the cliff top to the summit of Ber Dale, then onwards and downhill to the Quey and the lovely bay of Sand Wick. Head eastwards over the pastures of Sand Wick and you are soon back at Hillswick.

WALK 63

Esha Ness from Tangwick

Start/finish	At the car park at the Esha Ness lighthouse.
Grid ref	HU206785
Distance	14.5km/9 miles
Time	5–6 hours
Maps	OS Explorer 469; OS Landranger 3

A superb walk around the wild and high cliffs of Esha Ness.

The name **Esha Ness** comes from the Old Norse meaning Headland of Volcanic Rock. Black basalts and purple andesites make up the geology, and agates and amethysts can be found within these hard volcanic rocks.

Walk east from the lighthouse and along the top of Calder's Geo, where many seabirds will be nesting below your feet.

The Holes of Scraada

Calder's Geo is a huge void cutting into the cliffs at **Esha Ness**. Kittiwakes (known locally as waegs) and fulmars (maalies) nest here, while razorbills (sea craas) and guillemots (looms) can also be seen. Everyone's favourite seabird, the puffin (tammy norries) is also present, and shags (scarfs) nest at the bottom of the cliffs.

Walk around Calder's Geo and continue along what must surely be some of

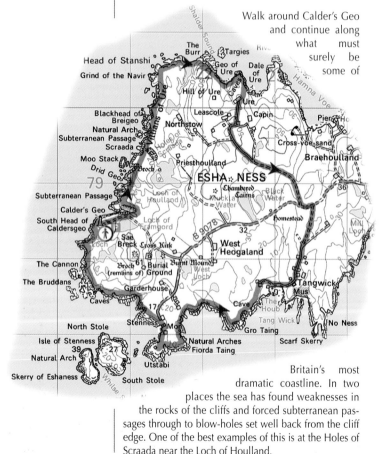

Britain's most dramatic coastline. In two places the sea has found weaknesses in the rocks of the cliffs and forced subterranean passages through to blow-holes set well back from the cliff edge. One of the best examples of this is at the Holes of Scraada near the Loch of Houlland.

The **Loch of Houlland** is a good place to see breeding Arctic terns (known hereabouts as scooty aalins) and great skuas (bonxies). These birds can be very aggressive if you approach their nests or young, so be warned!

The cliffs continue as you near the Head of Stanshi along the Villians of Ure (a fantastic name for a cliff top if ever there was one!), then to the Grind of Navir, a huge cleft in the coast where the sea has torn apart the rocks, then spat the boulders back out. Continue walking around the Geo of Ure and the Dale of Ure until you come to the tiny hamlet of Ure.

From Ure you head south on the lane, passing the tracks that lead off to the farms at Leascole, Capin and Northstow. Walk on until you come to a junction with the B9078. Turn left, then right within a couple of hundred metres, following the lane down to the hamlet of Tangwick. There is a superb museum in the hamlet, and it is well worth a visit.

The Grind of the Navir

173

Dore Holm

Tangwick Haa Museum has a fascinating display of local artefacts and photographs. Part of the exhibition is changed every year. All aspects of life in this remote part of Shetland are depicted here. The Haa itself was built as a home for the Cheyne family in the 17th century, and as such is one of the oldest buildings in this part of Shetland. The Cheyne family were lairds of the Tangwick Estate and other parts of Shetland.

From the museum drop down the lane around the back that leads westwards to the beach at the Houb, then continue along the low cliffs to Gro Taing and onwards to the natural coastal arches of Fiorda Taing.

Offshore lies the spectacular island of **Dore Holm**, with its huge natural arch. It is quite often called 'Horse and Man Rock', or 'Drinking Horse Rock' – this latter name seems much more fitting.

Around the bay to Utstabi, then the cliffs begin to rise again as you near Stenness, with the Isle of Stenness and Skerry of Eshaness lying just offshore. Continuing towards Eshaness itself the way leads across broken rocky ground around the Bruddans and the Cannon before you reach the lighthouse at the end of the B9078.

WALK 64

Ronas Hill – Highpoint of the Shetland Isles

Start/finish	On the A970, where the track goes westwards down to the houses at Voe (park sensibly so as to not block any gates or tracks).
Grid ref	HU338811
Distance	15.5km /9.6 miles
Time	5–6 hours
Maps	OS Explorer 469; OS Landranger 1 or 3
Note	Map and compass skills required.

Ronas Hill is not particularly high, rising to only 450m, but is the highest hill in Shetland, and second only to Ward Hill on Hoy (Orkney), making it the second highest peak in the Northern Isles.

A rare opportunity on Shetland to feel as though you are on a proper hill!

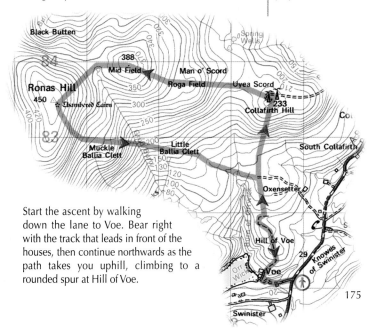

Start the ascent by walking down the lane to Voe. Bear right with the track that leads in front of the houses, then continue northwards as the path takes you uphill, climbing to a rounded spur at Hill of Voe.

A walker climbing Ronas Hill

Just above this spur the path becomes vague, and you should follow a bearing northwards up to a broad shoulder of the hill to the east of the headwaters of the Burn of Orrwick. From this flat shoulder continue northwards, over rough ground as it steepens towards the masts on Collafirth Hill.

Climb up the south side of the hill, gaining Collafirth Hill's summit at the masts at a point where a metalled lane comes up from the east at North Collafirth (this lane ends on Collafirth Hill and gives an easy approach to Ronas Hill – many people drive up to the end of the road, but of course that is cheating!).

Now turn westwards and drop down slightly to a boggy area known as Uyea Scord. This is a broad col between Collafirth Hill and the eastern flank of Ronas Hill. Head up the other side, going westwards, up the vague ridge of Roga Field until this merges with the rounded dome of Mid Field above.

Mid Field is separated from Ronas Hill by a col, known as Shurgie Scord. Once at the top of Mid Field, at 388m, drop down just south of west into this col. You'll see a small tarn down on the left, at the source of the Grud Burn. Now climb southwestwards to gain the small summit plateau of Ronas Hill. The summit is marked by an OS trig pillar at 450m, and there is an ancient chambered cairn nearby.

From the chambered cairn, which lies just southeast of the trig pillar, you can descend a short way to the south, then curve eastwards down the flank of the hill known as Muckle Ballia Clett. Follow a bearing eastwards across the Grud Burn until you are on the open slopes of Little Ballia Clett.

Do not descend too far, as the going lower down is hard. The route takes you further eastwards, over pathless terrain throughout, towards the head of Burn of Orrwick, and from here you can climb up to the east, out of the gully holding the burn, to gain the ridge you climbed earlier, above Hill of Voe.

Turn south down this ridge, descending to Hill of Voe itself, where you'll pick up the path you climbed from Voe. Retrace your steps southwards, down the path and out to your car on the A970.

WALK 65
The Beorgs of Skelberry

Start/finish	At North Roe village, on the A970.
Grid ref	HU366897
Distance	6.4km/4 miles
Time	3–4 hours
Maps	OS Explorer 469; OS Landranger 1 or 2

Start in North Roe village, just north of the school and chapel. Take the track for Greenfield on the left and follow this to the point where you cross the small stream flowing into the north side of Loch of Flugarth. You'll see the loch to your right.

Just over the stream the track splits and you should take the one to the left, climbing steadily to a broad bowl between the north ridge of Beorgs of Skelberry and the Hill of Sandvoe.

A short walk to a superb viewpoint – the Beorgs of Skelberry give extensive views over North Roe, and further afield to the islands of Yell Sound.

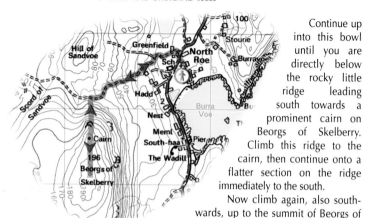

Continue up into this bowl until you are directly below the rocky little ridge leading south towards a prominent cairn on Beorgs of Skelberry. Climb this ridge to the cairn, then continue onto a flatter section on the ridge immediately to the south.

Now climb again, also southwards, up to the summit of Beorgs of Skelberry. The high point is marked by an Ordnance Survey trig point at 196m. The views to the northeast extend right across the wonderfully wild peninsula of North Roe, stretching as far as the Point of Fethaland, the most northerly tip of Mainland.

Descend to North Roe village by retracing your steps.

WALK 66

Point of Fethaland

Start/finish	At Isbister, north of North Roe village, on the A970.
Grid ref	HU372909
Distance	11km 6.8 miles/
Time	3–4 hours
Maps	OS Explorer 469; OS Landranger 1 or 2

This is a superb walk that should not be missed.

Start by going through a gate (marked 'Private Road' – this applies to cars only, not walkers). Turn right on a track heading for Houll, passing the cemetery, which has wooden grave 'stones'. The track passes to the right of the low hill of Lanchestoo, and you can make a diversion if you wish to climb to its summit at 130m.

Beyond Lanchestoo continue northwards to the east side of the Upper Loch of Setter, then walk on towards the coast, heading northwards to the Hill of Breibister. Here you will find yourself in a broad bowl overlooking the sea, and this is where you enter the peninsula of Fethaland.

Pass around the bay of Wick of Breibister, and head out towards the Point of Fethaland, across a narrow spit of rocks and boulders. Beyond the narrow neck you are on what is known as the Isle of Fethaland.

Way out across the open water to the north lie the various skerries of **Ramna Stacks**. The RSPB manages these outcrops as a reserve for nesting seabirds. Nearer at hand, on the Isle of Fethaland itself, there is about a score of ruined fishing boats, as well as a lighthouse overlooking Yellow Stack.

Enjoy exploring the little coves and stacks of Fethaland, then head back southwards, keeping to the west coast of the headland. As you leave Fethaland, don't forget to keep looking back at the marvellous view.

A gully cuts inland between Brunt Hill and Crogans, and you climb up this to a long, narrow tarn called Viga Water. Now head south across sheep pastures towards the west side

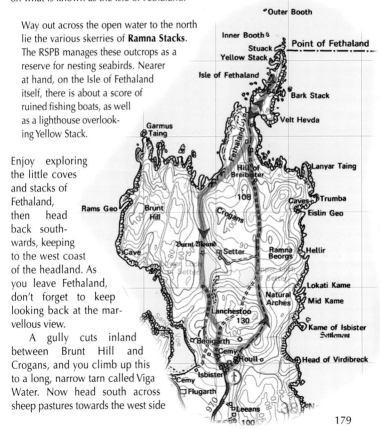

179

Superb scenery on Muckle Roe

of Lower Loch of Setter. Follow the western shore of the loch and you pick up a track heading south.

Follow this around the rocky western flank of Lanchestoo, then, as the track swings away to the southwest, down to the shore at Benigarth, turn off it and climb through pastures to the southeast, around the southwestern flanks of Lanchestoo. This will bring you out onto a track just above the hamlet of Isbister, and your car.

NORTHERN ISLANDS

WALK 67
Muckle Roe – South Ham

Start/finish	There is a small car-parking area on a grass verge at West Ayre at the end of the minor road running along the south side of the island. Follow the A970 north from Lerwick to Brae. In Brae turn left to Busta and on over the bridge that connects Mainland to the island of Muckle Roe.
Grid ref	HU322629
Distance	10.6km/6.5 miles
Time	5 hours
Maps	OS Explorer 469; OS Landranger 3

From West Ayre take the path marked 'Lighthouse'. This passes between the last two houses at the end of the road. Go westwards across a field and through a gate to a lovely bay. Cross a stream and take a track to the right (**Note** There is an obvious path climbing steeply immediately above the cliffs of Burki Taing. It's best to avoid this track and take the one to the right instead.)

The path climbs steadily to low-lying ling and bell heather moorland. Cross a stile, and then another one in a short distance. A handrail leads the way easily westwards, and then on to the southern tip of a little loch. Follow the path onwards and down to the outflow of Gilsa Water just below. ▶

Ignore the path that clings to the western shore of Gilsa Water. Instead, take the one to the left, once over the outflow. This climbs beneath lovely slabs of red granite, and leads easily to the yawning gulf in the cliffs to the west. This is the Hole of Hellier, beyond which you can walk easily up to the small lighthouse.

Many locals consider this walk, via the spectacular Hole of Hellier and a little lighthouse, to be the best in the whole of the Northern Isles.

Gilsa Water is a great place to look out for red-throated divers, but please do not disturb these birds during the nesting season.

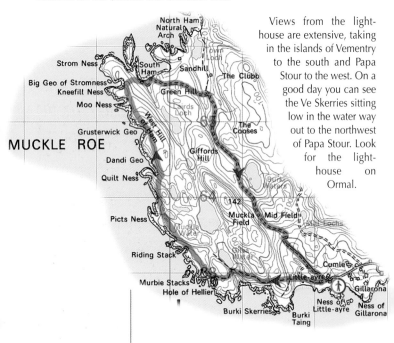

Views from the lighthouse are extensive, taking in the islands of Vementry to the south and Papa Stour to the west. On a good day you can see the Ve Skerries sitting low in the water way out to the northwest of Papa Stour. Look for the lighthouse on Ormal.

From the lighthouse head northwards across a rocky area and climb slightly to a small cairn of granite blocks. From here head around the slopes and descend carefully around the rocks to the top of the huge geo at Picts Ness. Cross a stream issuing from a tiny lochan and follow rough ground northwards to Dandi Geo.

Cross another small stream, this one falling in a small waterfall into Dandi Geo, and climb the rocky slopes of West Hill of Ham. Follow the broad ridge, taking in the superb views northwards towards Esha Ness. If you look carefully you can pick out the fantastic pink granite sea stacks of the Drongs away across St Magnus Bay.

Follow the ridge of West Hill of Ham and descend to a track at South Ham. Enjoy the lovely red sand beach here, then turn eastwards along the track. Follow this

A walker exploring Muckle Roe

Walking on Muckle Roe

around Green Hill, then head along it up the valley to the stream issuing from Burki Waters.

Continue over the pass between Muckla Field and Mid Field, keeping an eye out for great skuas, or bonxies as they are known around here. These large seabirds can be very territorial if you approach too close to their nests.

Just over the pass the track splits. Take the one to the right, dropping down the hill to a gate. Go through this and follow the track to the southeast and back to West Ayre.

WALK 68

Yell – the Old Haa and Heoga Ness

Start/finish	The Old Haa car park at Burravoe, on the island of Yell.
Grid ref	HU520794
Distance	4.2km/2.6 miles
Time	1–2 hours
Maps	OS Explorer 470; OS Landranger 3

The **Old Hall (Haa) of Brough** at Burravoe dates back to 1672, when it was built for local merchant Robert Tyrie. The museum houses lots of interesting artefacts and depicts what island life has been like over the years. Outside the haa is an archway bearing Tyrie's initials and the date 1672, while another interesting addition to the place is one of the propellers from a Catalina aeroplane that crashed on the Ward of Ottterswick on 19 January 1942. Seven of her 10 crew and passengers died.

A short coastal walk from the Old Haa of Brough at Burravoe, now a museum.

Once you've had a good look around the museum, head back up the road on foot. There's a chapel just north of the Old Haa, and this stands on a junction of minor roads. Turn right here and continue southeastwards down to the pier.

Once by the shore you can pick up a path that leads around the natural harbour of Burra Voe. Go northeastwards on this path, passing another pier as you approach the head of the voe. Now continue around the head and onto a narrow neck of land that connects the peninsula of Heoga Ness to the rest of Yell.

Walk southwestwards, keeping to the waterside as you reach the entrance to Burra Voe, with the voe itself to your right throughout. The entrance is marked by the headland of Outer Virdik, and from there you continue around Heoga Ness, passing the rocks of Gold Skerry as you walk along Vats Wick bay.

Now the route takes you around the head of Cumlins before arriving at a small promontory called the Rett. The coast stretches northwards in a rocky curve, around to the Scarves and the beautiful bay of Whal Wick. Seals often haul out onto the shelving rock here. North of the bay lies Windi Clett and the rough headland – almost an island – known as North Taing.

Beyond North Taing the coast cuts back towards the west, and you must follow it to the narrow neck of land known as Helia Dale. Cross this to the west, and pick up the path around Burra Voe that you walked along earlier. Retrace your steps back to the Old Haa.

WALK 69
Yell – Ward of Otterswick

Start/finish	The chapel by the roadside below Hamnavoe.
Grid ref	HU495803
Distance	12.9km/8 miles
Time	6–7 hours
Maps	OS Explorer 470; OS Landranger 1 and 2
Note	Map and compass skills required

This is a delightful moorland walk to the highest point of the island of Yell.

Walk northwestwards along the road from the chapel at Hamnavoe. The road leads to a bridge over the Burn of Arisdale. Just before the bridge a track leaves the road on the right and you should follow this up the wide, rough dale to the farm at Arisdale.

Up the valley here you pass the **Catalina Memorial**, commemorating those lost in an air crash on the Ward of Otterswick on 19 January 1942. Seven of the 10 crew and passengers died, and at the Old Haa Museum in Burravoe you'll see one of the propellers from the aeroplane.

From Arisdale a steep climb up to the northeast leads onto the broad ridge of Hill of Arisdale. Climb up through heather and moorland grasses to the summit of Yell's highest hill, at 210m. The views from the Hill of Arisdale are spectacular. To the east you can see the hills of Fetlar rising out of the sea, while the rocky lumps to the southeast are the Out Skerries. Westwards the bald plateau of Ronas Hill forms a bare knoll rising over the surrounding moorland. Ronas Hill is the highest point on Shetland.

Continue northeastwards along the ridge to the Ordnance Survey trig pillar at Ward of Otterswick, at 205m. A little to the north lies a large cairn. Walk on to this then return to the trig point. Descend to the southeast, into a wide and boggy col where a little tarn sits.

Now continue to the southeast, barely climbing at all to reach the Hill of Canisdale at 159m. Southeast again, across more rough and boggy moorland, lies the low ridge of Atli's Hill at 127m. Drop down a short way into another wide col, then climb up to the summit of Atli's Hill.

Now the going becomes a little easier and more defined, although still without a path underfoot. There is a ridge running southwards from Atli's Hill, curving gradually to the southwest and ending on the flat-topped spur of Beaw Field. Follow this ridge throughout, finally descending off the southwest side to a sheepfold and track end.

Turn left, southwards along this track, bearing right at the junction just above Hamnavoe. Cross a ford on the left to reach the end of the

187

public road in Hamnavoe, and follow this road south-wards to a junction. Turn right and walk downhill slightly towards the chapel where you parked.

WALK 70
Yell – the White Wife

Start/finish	The pub at the junction of minor roads, just east of the B9081, north of Otterswick.
Grid ref	HU519863
Distance	6.5km/4 miles
Time	2–3 hours
Maps	OS Explorer 470; OS Landranger 1 or 2

This is a lovely walk to one of Shetland's most visited memorials, the White Wife of Otterswick.

The walk starts at a pub beneath Corn Hill, although this ramshackle building doesn't look anything at all like it when you get there. Turn right and walk along the lane to Midgarth. Walk along the dead-end road to a car park and a stile on the right.

Otterswick Bay

The White Wife

Go over the stile and follow the path beneath the farm buildings at Queyon. The path passes down through fields then onto moorland. It leads easily down to the coast at the White Wife overlooking the bay of Otterswick.

On the shore at Otterswick there is a prominent figure-head known as the **White Wife**. This came from the steel barque Bohus. Bohus was built in 1892, but on a fateful day, 26 April 1924, she sailed under Captain Hugh Ferdinand Blume around the east side of Yell. She was caught in a terrific storm off Otters Wick, and soon ran aground onto the rocks. Three young sailors died as the ship broke up. The White Wife is the figurehead from the Bohus, and she now stands looking across the bay where the ship was wrecked and the men perished.

Walk onwards around the coast to the Ness of Queyon, looking for signs of wildlife as you go.

The rocky shore here is a good place to see **seals**, and they are often out on Black Skerry, while **otters** are also occasionally seen here. Out in the bay you might also see common **porpoises** feeding on shoals of surface-feeding fish.

From the Ness of Queyon turn northwards towards the broad bay of Salt Wick, then around a little knab to Haa of Aywick. The Haa, an old house, lies just back from the coast, and from there you can follow a track northwestwards out to the hamlet of Aywick.

Follow the road westwards through the hamlet, reaching a junction and bearing left. This road climbs over open moorland, and soon leads you back to the pub beneath Corn Hill.

WALK 71

Yell – Stuis of Graveland

Start/finish	The end of the minor road at Efstigarth, parking sensibly before you reach the farm buildings.
Grid ref	HU463927
Distance	11.7km/7.3 miles
Time	3–4 hours
Maps	OS Explorer 470; OS Landranger 1 and 2
Note	Map and compass skills required.

A stunning walk to a remote peninsula on Yell, overlooking the deep fjord of Whale Firth.

Start by walking along the lane towards the farm at Efstigarth. Before you reach the boundary just before the burn, turn uphill to the west, climbing over the rough moorland to the ridge of Canning Knowe. Bear off to the north along this broad ridge, curving around to the northwest slightly to gain the summit of Virdi Field at 143m.

Apart from the seawater that surrounds the peninsula upon which Virdi Field is the highest hill – Whale Firth to the east and Yell Sound to the west – there are lots of lovely freshwater lochs dotted around the moorland.

Immediately west of Virdi Field lie the Cro Waters, a collection of three large tarns, while to the northeast the Loch of Graveland huddles beneath the ridge.

Drop down off the ridge of Virdi Field to the northeast, aiming for a col with a sprinkling of little pools on its flattest part. Now climb to the northwest, gaining the fine summit of Stany Hill, perched just back from the cliffs of Norther Geo. The summit is at 134m.

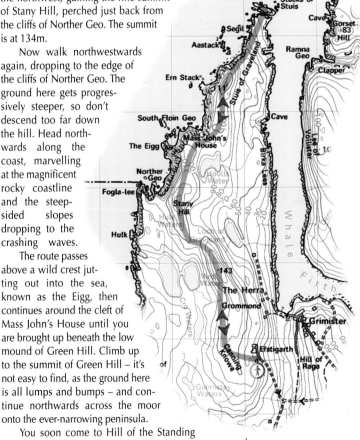

Now walk northwestwards again, dropping to the edge of the cliffs of Norther Geo. The ground here gets progressively steeper, so don't descend too far down the hill. Head northwards along the coast, marvelling at the magnificent rocky coastline and the steep-sided slopes dropping to the crashing waves.

The route passes above a wild crest jutting out into the sea, known as the Eigg, then continues around the cleft of Mass John's House until you are brought up beneath the low mound of Green Hill. Climb up to the summit of Green Hill – it's not easy to find, as the ground here is all lumps and bumps – and continue northwards across the moor onto the ever-narrowing peninsula.

You soon come to Hill of the Standing Stone, with its summit at 111m giving a fine viewpoint

191

from which to appreciate the Aastack across the bay and Ern Stack looking back along the coast.

Now continue, to the northeast this time, keeping the coast close by on the left, until you get a superb view of the natural arch of Segil. This lies just before you reach the tip of the peninsula of the Stuis of Graveland. At the very tip there is a narrow neck connecting the Nev of Stuis to the main island. You can scramble out onto this for superb views all around.

For the return to your car, either retrace your steps, or follow the high ground over Hill of the Standing Stone, Green Hill, Stany Hill and Virdi Field, without recourse to the cliff edge overlooking Yell Sound to the west.

The Fishermen's Memorial at the Gloup on Yell (Walk 72)

WALK 72

Yell – the Gloup and North Neaps

Start/finish	At the Gloup Memorial.
Grid ref	HP506045
Distance	13.5km/8.4 miles
Time	2–3 hours
Maps	OS Explorer 470; OS Landranger 1

Start from the Gloup Memorial and drop downhill slightly from the car park, following a path to the south-west. Don't drop all the way to the shore, but instead climb a stile and traverse along the grassy slopes, overlooking the long and narrow inlet of Gloup Voe.

A short walk around the magnificent sandy cove of Gloup Voe.

The **Fishermen's Memorial** at Gloup is a stone sculpture looking out to sea. It commemorates the 58 men who died in July 1881 when their boats were overcome by a great storm while they were out deep-sea fishing. The names of the men, and their boats, as well as where they lived, are all listed on the memorial. The memorial was erected in 1981.

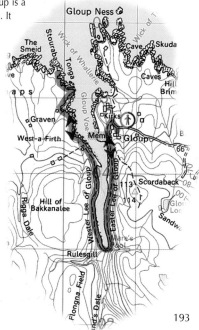

Continue walking southwards, along the flanks of Easter Lee of Gloup, until you reach the head of the inlet. Here the path takes you right down to the water level, at least when the tide is in.

Cross a burn here and keep along the shore, turning around at the head of the bay and continuing back along the Wester Lee of Gloup.

WALK 73

Unst – Valla Field

Start/finish	Park sensibly at Westing.
Grid ref	HP572061
Distance	8km/5 miles
Time	2–3 hours
Maps	OS Explorer 470; OS Landranger 1
Note	Map and compass skills required.

A wild moorland walk on the west side of the island.

Start by walking along the lane from Westing to its end beyond New Gord. Here a track continues out onto the open moorland to the north of Breck of Newgord, and you should walk northwards across the moor to the coast at Collaster. There is a wonderfully wild headland here, known as the Ness of Collaster.

Walk around the Ness of Collaster until you reach a burn plunging from a small cliff onto the beach below. This burn drains the tiny Loch of Collaster. Now continue around the coast, passing the magnificent Bogligarths Geo, then head inland to the northeast to the freshwater Loch of Bogligarths.

The coast continues northwards to Hagdales Ness, and you follow it around deeply in-cut Longa Geo, then out onto the Ness itself. From Hagdales Ness walk eastwards, climbing steeply to gain the moorland ridge of Ward of Houlland.

This is all **superb moorland terrain**, and you might see nesting dunlin, golden plover, curlew and whimbrel on these wild moors. Also, keep a look out on the freshwater lochs for nesting loon, or red-throated divers, as they are more commonly called.

To the immediate southwest of Ward of Houlland the ridge runs quite broadly, and then in a short way, from the top of Hagmark, turns southwards and becomes more pronounced, with steep ground falling away to the coast at Collaster to the west.

Keep to the top edge of this steep ground, gaining superb views down to the coast as you walk southwards to Valla Field. First you'll reach the summit of Byre of Scord, which at 216m is the high point of the ridge. This is marked by an OS trig pillar. To the south from the trig point there is another knoll, known as Berry Knowe, before the narrower ridge of Valla Field itself. To the east of the ridge here the Longa Water is a beautiful spot.

Drop down the south side of Valla Field, then pick up a track continuing southwards. Follow this for half a mile then leave it to descend to the west, steeply at first. Drop down to Gossa Water, then gain the fields of Westings and walk through these as skylarks rise at your feet.

Walk westwards through the fields to regain the minor road at Westings, and the end of a wonderfully wild walk

WALK 74

Unst – Keen of Hamar

Start/finish	The car park signposted from the road between Baltasound and Haroldswick.
Grid ref	HP642095
Distance	1.9km/1.2 miles
Time	1–2 hours
Maps	OS Explorer 470; OS Landranger 1

This is an unusual walk, taking in the stony headland of the Keen of Hamar National Nature Reserve.

The **Keen of Hamar** is a paradise for any naturalist, particularly if you are interested in flora. The botanical interest of this low headland was first recognised in 1837, when a young lad from nearby Buness at Baltasound started making some unusual discoveries. Thomas Edmondston, at the remarkable age of 12, came across a new type of Arctic chickweed (Cerastium nigrescens arcticum), now known as Edmonston's chickweed, or Shetland mouse-ear. This beautiful plant occurs only at the Keen of Hamar, except for a few colonies of a narrow-leaved form that grow on nearby Muckle Heog and Crussa Field.

From the car park you will see a corridor running between fences to the north. This was specially created as a 'cattle crossing', so that animals could be taken from one side of the reserve to another without damaging the fragile ecosystem. You can use this to begin your own explorations.

Head north along the corridor, then, as you drop down towards the Wick of Hagdale, a large bay on the north side of the Keen of Hamar, take to the coast to the right. This contours at first, then, as the cliffs rise to your left, you climb up to the highest point of the reserve at 87m.

Stone stripes can be seen running across the bare north-facing slopes of the reserve here. These are formed through the sorting of stones by size following the repeated freeze/thawing action of water in the soil. In Britain this process is usually associated with high mountains such as the Cairngorms National Park, or the peaks of Blencathra and Helvellyn in the Lake District National Park. However, at the Keen of Hamar, where there is little vegetation to hold the soil together, these stone stripes occur at just 50m above sea level. Experiments have shown that where the ground surface has been disturbed, the stripes may reform in a single winter.

From the high point of the reserve, head westwards alongside a fence. This leads down to the corridor that will take you southwards back to your car.

Traditional boat building at Haroldswick, on the north side of Keen of Hamar

197

WALK 75

Unst – the Horns of Hagmark

Start/finish	There is a car park at Norwick. Follow the B9087 through Haroldswick and on to RAF Saxa Vord. Continue northeastwards to Norwick and park down by the shore.
Grid ref	HP651145
Distance	8.4km/5.2 miles
Time	3–4 hours
Maps	OS Explorer 470; OS Landranger 1

A lonely walk around the coast to the east of Haroldswick. The destination is Hill of Clibberswick via the spectacular cliffs of the Horns of Hagmark.

From the car-parking area near the beach at Norwick, head back along the lane to a junction. Turn left here and follow the dead-end road to Millfield, passing the cemetery and old kirk on the left. Beyond Millfield a fence leads out onto the open moor, and you can head eastwards towards the low cliffs at Burgar.

Look out for nesting shags, kittiwakes and fulmars on the cliffs hereabouts, while great skuas and Arctic skuas patrol the moor.

Turn right along the coast, following the rising ground with the cliffs to your left. Walk around the magnificent bay of Girr Wick, crossing the stream of Girr Dale immediately afterwards, then continue climbing gently around to Valtoes. Keep a look out for spectacular rock pinnacles just offshore, including the North Stane and Ship Stack.

From Valtoes the cliff line runs roughly in a southerly direction. Follow this, climbing more steeply now, until you come to a broad platform on the left. Here great sweeping cliffs plunge down into the sea overlooked by Hagmark Stack. This area of spires and pinnacles is known as the Horns of Hagmark, and it is one of the finest sections of coastline on Unst.

A little further along the cliffs is the high point of the walk, the Hill of Clibberswick at 160m. The summit is set right on the very edge of the cliffs, and is marked by an

Ordnance Survey trig point, as well as the remains of an ancient cairn.

Continue southwards, downhill now, until the cliffs curve slightly to the southeast and you reach another flat area. This is known as the Giant, and overlooks Hinda Stack, the whole craggy hillside being the scenic equal to the Horns of Hagmark to the north.

Now the route drops down further, descending to the south again, and passing above Mooa Stack before bringing you out on the southern tip of this wonderful headland. This is called the Nev, and immediately to the west this small promontory is cut off from the rest of the headland by a great cleft. This cleft is known as Rurra Geo, and it is worth walking right up to the edge for the amazing views into its depths.

Now walk northwards, keeping Rurra Geo close by to your left. Climb uphill and around the cleft, then down the other side to pick up the coast again. Head along the coast to the northwest, passing by His Geo and the fine architectural natural arch of Cross Geo.

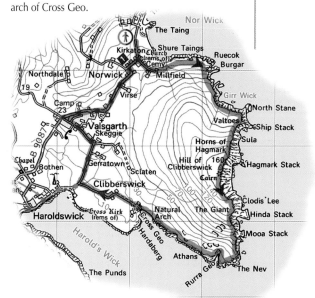

Continue around the geo until you reach the remains of Cross Kirk, then head northwestwards along a track to pick up the end of a minor road at Clibberswick.

> Here the fields are alive with wildflowers in the summer, and there are lots of **nesting birds** close by too. Look out for curlews, whimbrel, snipe, skylark, meadow pipit and twite.

Head out along the lane from Clibberswick. You are soon clear of the few houses of the hamlet, then come to a road junction. Turn right and follow the lane up to Valsgarth, where the RAF Saxa Vord base is. Turn right along the B9087 and follow this road back to your car at Norwick.

WALK 76
Unst – Wick of Skaw

Start/finish	You can park at the end of the road at the Haa, reached by turning left at the junction in Norwick and following the lane over the moor and down to Skaw.
Grid ref	HP657163
Distance	1.6km/1 miles
Time	1 hour
Maps	OS Explorer 470; OS Landranger 1
Note	The outbuildings at Skaw – they are made up of overturned boats.

A short stroll from the beautiful beach at Skaw, which can reasonably claim to be the furthest north in the British Isles, as can the Haa at Skaw.

Start by heading down to the beach from the car park. Enjoy a stroll around the beach, looking for wading birds down by the shore, and marvelling at the long rollers coming in off the North Atlantic.

Continue by walking up into the northwest corner of the beach, then climb up onto the grassy slope above. Here you pick up a track. Turn right along it and follow it out onto the headland to look across a narrow passage, the Ham Sound, to the islands of Holm of Skaw.

Walk anti-clockwise around the headland, passing the wide gulf of the Forn Geo, before making your way out to the promontory known as Houlls-nef. On the northern tip of this is a fine rock spire known as Score Stack, and fulmars can be seen nesting here.

The wonderful bay at Wick of Skaw

Walk southwestwards along the coast for a quarter of a mile, then head south over short-cropped grasses and flowers to pick up a track. This leads southwards towards the track you walked out along earlier. Turn right along this track to return to Skaw.

201

WALK 77

Unst – Hermaness National Nature Reserve

Start/finish	There is a dedicated car park at the Ness, just above the lighthouse shore station. As you approach, do not turn right down to the lighthouse, but veer off left to reach the car park.
Grid ref	HP612149
Distance	9km/5.6 miles
Time	3 –4 hours
Maps	OS Explorer 470; OS Landranger 1

The walk to the cliffs at Hermaness and back over Hermaness Hill is one of my favourites on the Northern Isles during summer – a must for anyone with a love of wild places and wildlife in the raw.

Start by walking down from the car park along the lane to the lighthouse shore station. There is a small visitor centre here, which is well worth a brief visit. Return to the car park, then pass through the kissing gate at the far end.

This leads out onto a good track that takes you northwards alongside a fence.

The terrain hereabouts is quite rough. This is **typical Unst moorland**, with heather and peat hags stretching in all directions.

The visitor centre at Hermaness

Within half a mile the path drops down to cross a stream – the delightfully named Burn of Winnaswarta Dale. Cross the burn and go left, still on the obvious path.

HERMANESS

The moorland at Hermaness is one of the main sites in Britain – well actually in the world – for breeding great skuas. These pirates of the air nest on the open moorland here, and can be very aggressive if you approach them when they have eggs or young. During the summer months you simply can't help but see them in their hundreds, as the Hermaness National Nature Reserve is the third largest breeding colony in the world.

You should also look out for the slimmer and more agile Arctic skuas that also nest on the moors here. These acrobatic birds will also defend their eggs and young with vigour, and are more than happy to swoop and dive-bomb humans. Arctic skuas can be seen here in two different colour phases. The most obvious is chocolate brown, but you will also see some that are creamy-white underneath. This difference does not denote male or female, as either sex can be seen in both colour phases.

As you climb out of the gully holding the burn, there is a junction in the path. Take the left-hand fork, which goes straight ahead alongside the burn on its north side.

As you climb up alongside the burn you become more and more aware of the presence of skuas all around.

The climb alongside the burn is gentle, and although boggy in places, the managers of the reserve, Scottish Natural Heritage (SNH), have laid a number of duck-boards to ease your passage.

As the angle eases even further, you come abruptly to the cliff edge at Toolie, and below you the crags drop

PUFFINS

A puffin at Hermaness National Nature Reserve

Twenty-five thousand pairs of puffins breed along the cliffs at Hermaness, and this is one of the best places in the world to get in among them. If you edge up to their burrows, steadily but slowly, you can sit just feet away and watch them emerging to head out to sea. If you wait long enough you will also be treated to the wonderful sight of them returning to the nest with their bills stuffed full of sand eels.

Puffins have a specially adapted bill, so that they can catch a large number of sand eels in one dive. The bill hinges in an odd way, so that when open, the edges remain parallel to each other. This way the bird can catch more fish without losing those already firmly held.

Puffins are remarkable in many more ways. One particularly notable fact is that the chicks leave the nest at night, and are flightless at this early stage in their development. However, they are so light – nothing more than a bundle of feather really – that they just bounce down the cliffs into the sea without coming to any harm. They then head off into the North Atlantic to find their parents, and to learn how to fish from the surface.

away dramatically into the broiling surf. It is worth spending some time here sitting and watching the fantastic spectacle of thousands of seabirds coming in from and going out to the sea.

You can walk in either direction along the rugged coastline from Toolie. However, this walk takes you in a circuit to the northeast, over Hermaness Hill. Having said that, many visitors to the reserve take a stroll southwards for a short way, to enjoy the views down into the coves, and to see if they can spot 'Albert the Albatross'!

ALBERT THE ALBATROSS

For a number of years a black-browed albatross was seen hanging out with the thousands of breeding gannets that returned each summer to Scotland. Between 1967 and 1969 one had been present on Bass Rock in the Forth of Firth, then from 1972 until the mid-1990s there was another, possibly the same bird, over at Hermaness. Even prior to the individual turning up on Bass Rock in 1967, there had been yet another albatross – and many people feel that it is likely to have been Albert – in Iceland during July of 1966.

These huge birds are found in the deep south of the Southern Ocean, and don't usually venture north of the equator. However, Albert, as he inevitably became known, was thought to have strayed too far north, and got mixed up with a band of gannets who were heading up to Scotland to breed. He joined the throng and stayed with them for many years, even trying his best to mate with any female gannet that happened to take his fancy.

For a while back in the 1970s, ornithologists speculated that Albert might actually have been a female, because from 1976 onwards it built a nest at Saito, just south of Toolie at Hermaness, but never laid eggs. However, it is now known that with black-browed albatrosses both sexes take part in the nest-building process, and it is agreed that if Albert was female, infertile eggs would most certainly have been laid during this period.

Albert was last seen at Hermaness on 7 July 1995, which, assuming that he was the same individual seen in Iceland, would have made him at least 32 years old back then. Then, from 2005, another – or possibly the same – albatross turned up on the remote islands of Sula Sgeir and North Rona, way out in the North Atlantic. If this huge-winged bird on Sula Sgeir is our old friend, he would now be at least 41 years old, and still going strong.

Muckle Flugga off the northern tip of Hermaness

Walk northeastwards along the coast, passing the remarkable scenery of the cliffs to your left. Within a short way you start to get good views of the islet and lighthouse of Muckle Flugga. Just up the slope from the cliff edge is a path that contours northwards, and you should follow this to a point where it turns uphill to the right. Ahead, across the water, lie the skerries of Muckle Flugga.

The **lighthouse on Muckle Flugga** was first used on 11 October 1854, and was designed by Thomas and David Stevenson. Thomas Stevenson was Robert Louis Stevenson's father.

The skerries around the main rock of Muckle Flugga – Little Flugga, Cliff Skerry, Tipta Skerry, Pulsa Stack, Rumblings and Vesta Skerry – together hold a huge and important breeding colony of gannets.

The climb up to Hermaness Hill is straightforward. It takes you via a peaty path eastwards, then curves around to the southeast to reach the summit at 200m.

There are a number of **pools** near the summit that occasionally hold a breeding pair of red-throated divers. Dunlin, snipe and red grouse can also be seen on the moorland hereabouts.

The path now descends the broad flanks to the south, taking you across the open moorland of Sothers Brecks. From there it begins to drop down the eastern side of the hill, cutting a course towards the bottom end of Burn of Winnaswarta Dale. Here, just as it reaches the side of the burn, it joins the track you took outwards earlier in the day.

Turn left along the track and retrace your steps to the car park.

WALK 78
Fetlar – Lamb Hoga

Start/finish	There is a large car-parking area in the machair dunes below the manse and chapel at Tresta on the island of Fetlar.
Grid ref	HU607904
Distance	4.8km/3 miles
Time	1–2 hours
Maps	OS Explorer 470; OS Landranger 1 or 2

The **Lamb Hoga** peninsula is formed from a band of gneiss, which is one of the reasons it still exists – gneiss is a very hard rock.

Start by walking southwest from the parking area, either along the Sand of Tresta or along the wonderful machair dunes that separate the sea from the freshwater loch of Papil Water.

Papil Water is a great place to see great skuas in the summer. Many of these birds, otherwise known as

The finger of raised land known as Lamb Hoga is the long southwestern peninsula of the island of Fetlar.

The Wick of Tresta and Lamb Hoga on Fetlar

bonxies, gather on the loch to feed, and also to wash and preen.

At the far end of the beach a path starts climbing up the flanks of Lamb Hoga. Follow this path to the south, gaining height as you skirt around the lower slopes of Fitsyi Field. The path is very distinct and easy to follow.

Lamb Hoga has **two tops** along its length. Fitsyi Field overlooks the bay at Tresta, while the higher summit, known as Gillis Field, rises to 116m.

The path passes over a col between Fitsyi Field and Gillis Field, and as you approach the col between the two, where the gradient eases, there is a junction. Take the path to the left, aiming for the obvious OS trig point on the summit of Gillis Field.

Lamb Hoga is very **peaty**, and for many years was the site where locals came to dig peat for their fires. The stooks were piled up to dry in the wind and sun, then ponies would be taken up onto the moor to 'flit' the fuel back to the villages, ready for the winter.

The walk ends at Gillis Field, from where you retrace your steps to your car.

WALK 79
Fetlar – Funzie Ness

Start/finish	Park at the northeastern end of Loch of Funzie, on the side of the minor road by the cattle-grid.
Grid ref	HU656900
Distance	5.9km/3.7 miles
Time	2–3 hours
Maps	OS Explorer 470; OS Landranger 1 and 2

Funzie Ness lies at the southeastern end of Fetlar, south of the B9088. Start at the cattle-grid overlooking the northeastern end of the Loch of Funzie (pronounced 'finnie').

This walk takes in the Loch of Funzie, home to the tiny red-necked phalarope.

The coast at Funzie Ness

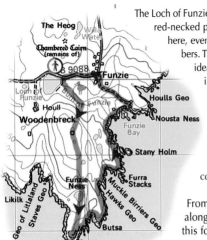

The Loch of Funzie is famous for a very small bird. The red-necked phalarope has its British stronghold here, even though it only nests in small numbers. The mires around the loch provide an ideal nesting habitat for these tiny wading birds, so much so that a third of the British population can be found here during the summer months. Once the eggs are laid, the female leaves all the incubation and chick-rearing duties to the male, so he is the drabber in colour of the two sexes.

From the end of the loch a path skirts alongside a stone wall on the left. Follow this for a short distance, then head south across the open moorland of the Crooans. Pass a large cairn on the high ground of the moor, then drop down to the south towards Croo Water, passing over pathless terrain. The going here is easy, as the terrain is mainly short-cropped grass and broken rocks.

South of Croo Water there is a fine little peninsula, the Snap. Walk out to the tip of the Snap to enjoy views over to the distant outline of the Out Skerries.

Now turn to the northeast and follow the coast, watching fulmars coasting by as you go. The first big feature along the coast is the headland of Butsa, then a series of coves present themselves. The first is Hawks Geo, then comes Muckle Birriers Geo, before a fine, jutting-out promontory overlooking Furra Stacks. To the north lies Funzie Bay, and you can walk right around this wide cove, keeping to the top of the low cliffs as you go.

On the north side of the bay, before the headland of Nousta Ness that forms the outer point of the bay on its north side, there is an old house, the Haa of Funzie. A track runs from the end of the public road down to the haa, and you should gain this and follow it to the northwest, passing to the left of the haa itself.

Continue along the track until you reach the end of the public road at Funzie. A short stroll to the west will take you to the cattle-grid at Loch of Funzie, and the end of this fine walk.

WALK 80
Fetlar – Vord Hill

Start/finish	Park at the end of the dead-end road at Dale of Baela, near to the school, but without blocking any entrances.
Grid ref	HU626913
Distance	7.2km/4.5 miles
Time	3–4 hours
Maps	OS Explorer 470; OS Landranger 1 or 2
Note	Map and compass skills required.

Start by heading north to the end of the lane beyond the school. There is an enclosure ahead, with the old farm buildings at Setter inside. At the entrance to the enclosure a path goes off to the right and left. Take the one to the right, running along the outside of the Riggin of Setter enclosure.

The path leads out onto the open moorland of Smugga of Setter, and once there you can head northeast over untracked moor to the broad ridge of Rooin, coming down from Vord Hill way off to the northwest.

Turn along the broad ridge, climbing gently as you ascend Vord Hill. Continue to the northwest throughout, all the way to the summit at 159m. The summit is adorned by an Ordnance Survey triangulation pillar, and a scattering of ancient cairns. The highest point lies just northeast of the trig pillar.

This area of Fetlar was for many years the scene of much activity and excitement among **birdwatchers**. The rough moorland around Vord Hill used to hold

A rough and remote wilderness walk to the highest point of the island of Fetlar, Vord Hill.

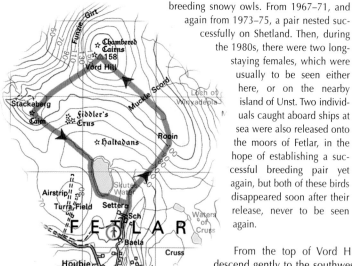

breeding snowy owls. From 1967–71, and again from 1973–75, a pair nested successfully on Shetland. Then, during the 1980s, there were two long-staying females, which were usually to be seen either here, or on the nearby island of Unst. Two individuals caught aboard ships at sea were also released onto the moors of Fetlar, in the hope of establishing a successful breeding pair yet again, but both of these birds disappeared soon after their release, never to be seen again.

From the top of Vord Hill descend gently to the southwest, gaining a very broad and open ridge leading towards the distant rocky outcrops of Stackaberg. This wonderfully wild little hill also has ancient cairns about its summit.

Now turn to the southwest, dropping down above a wall, and continuing until you reach the north side of a burn. This leads across a wet and sometimes boggy mire to the northwestern shore of Skutes Water, and once there you can walk around the loch in either direction until you are at the southeastern end.

Now continue to the southeast again, walking over pathless terrain until you hit the enclosure at Riggin of Setter. Turn south and regain the end of the public road at the school in Dale of Baela.

APPENDIX
Route summary table

ORKNEY

Walk		Island	Distance (km/miles)	Map	Time (hours)
1	Mull Head and the Brough of Deerness	Orkney Mainland	7.2/4.5	Explorer 461	3–4
2	The Deerness Memorial	Orkney Mainland	7.2/4.5	Explorer 461	3–4
3	Wideford Hill	Orkney Mainland	5.1/3.2	Explorer 463	2–3
4	Ward Hill	Orkney Mainland	9.6/6	Explorer 463	3–4
5	Ring of Brodgar and Stones of Stenness	Orkney Mainland	10/6.2	Explorer 463	3–4
6	Skara Brae, Yesnaby and Stromness	Orkney Mainland	26.2/16.3	Explorer 463	8–10
7	Marwick Head and the Kitchener Memorial	Orkney Mainland	9.6/6	Explorer 463	3–4
8	Brough Head	Orkney Mainland	2.6/1.6	Explorer 463	1–2
9	Loch of Hundland and Mid Hill	Orkney Mainland	22.5/14	Explorer 463	6–7
10	Fibla Fiold and Mid Tooin	Orkney Mainland	11.4/7.1	Explorer 463	3–4
11	Hoxa Head	South Ronaldsay	1.9/1.2	Explorer 461	1
12	Hundra Reef	Burray	5.4/3.4	Explorer 461	1–2
13	Heldale Water and Tor Ness	Hoy	17.7/11	Explorer 462	6–7
14	The Old Man of Hoy, St John's Head and Cuilags from Rackwick	Hoy	18.1/11.3	Explorer 462	7–8
15	Ward Hill From Moaness	Hoy	15.7/9.8	Explorer 462	5–6
16	Knitchen Hill and Trumland	Rousay	4.8/3	Explorer 464	2–3
17	Mid Howe Broch and Westness	Rousay	6.4/4	Explorer 464	2–3
18	Suso Burn and Kierfea Hill	Rousay	7.7/4.8	Explorer 464	3–4
19	Faraclett Head	Rousay	3.7/2.3	Explorer 464	1–2
20	Ward Hill and War Ness	Eday	3.9/2.4	Explorer 465	2–3
21	Noup Hill and Red Head	Eday	8/5	Explorer 465	2–3
22	Fers Ness and West Side	Eday	7.2/4.5	Explorer 465	2–3
23	Inga Ness to Noup Head	Westray	17.2/11	Explorer 464	6–7
24	Mull Head and North Hill	Papa Westray	3.2/2	Explorer 464	2–3
25	North Ronaldsay Coastal Traverse	North Ronaldsay	11.5/7.2	Explorer 465	4–5

SHETLAND

Walk		Island	Distance (km/miles)	Map	Time (hours)
26	Jarlshof and Sumburgh Head	South Mainland Shetland	4/2.5	Explorer 466	2–3
27	Ness of Burgi	South Mainland Shetland	3.25/2	Explorer 466	1–2
28	Fitful Head	South Mainland Shetland	9/5.5	Explorer 466	4–5
29	Fora Ness	South Mainland Shetland	5/3	Explorer 466	2–3
30	St Ninian's Isle over the Tombolo	St Ninian's Isle	5/3	Explorer 466	2–3
31	Taing of Maywick	South Mainland Shetland	1.5/1	Explorer 466	1
32	Deepdale from Maywick	South Mainland Shetland	9.5/6	Explorer 466	4–5
33	Sandwick to No Ness	South Mainland Shetland	6.5/4	Explorer 466	2–3
34	The Helli Ness Peninsula	South Mainland Shetland	4.8/3	Explorer 466	2
35	Muskna Field from Wester Quarff	South Mainland Shetland	5.6/3.5	Explorer 466	2
36	Scrae Field and the White Stone of Toufield	South Mainland Shetland	9.6/6	Explorer 466	3–4
37	Ward Hill	Fair Isle	5.6/3.5	Explorer 466	2
38	Malcolm's Head	Fair Isle	2.9/1.8	Explorer 466	1
39	West Coast traverse	Fair Isle	16/10	Explorer 466	8
40	Mousa Broch and RSPB Reserve	Mousa	2.8/1.75	Explorer 466	3
41	Kettla Ness	West Burra	7.4/4.6	Explorer 466	3
42	Houss Ness and the Ward of Symbister	East Burra	5.6/3.5	Explorer 466	2
43	Lerwick Old Town and the Nab	Central Mainland Shetland	2.5/1.5	Explorer 466	1
44	Scalloway to the Hill of Burwick	Central Mainland Shetland	8.8/5.5	Explorer 466	4
45	Fora Ness	Central Mainland Shetland	7.7/4.8	Explorer 467	3
46	Easter Skeld to Skelda Ness	Central Mainland Shetland	13.7/8.5	Explorer 467	4–5
47	Scord of Brouster	Central Mainland Shetland	0.4/0.2	Explorer 467	0.5

Walk		Island	Distance (km/miles)	Map	Time (hours)
48	Staneydale Temple	Central Mainland Shetland	2.4/1.5	Explorer 467	1
49	Mu Ness to Deepdale over Sandness Hill	Central Mainland Shetland	13.2/8.2	Explorer 467	5
50	Ness of Noonsborough	Central Mainland Shetland	6.9/4.3	Explorer 467	3
51	Scalla Field and the Butter Stone	Central Mainland Shetland	9/5.6	Explorer 467	3
52	North Nesting Coast	Central Mainland Shetland	12.8/8	Explorer 467 and 468	4–5
53	Daal to the Sneck Ida Smallie	Foula	8.3/5.2	Explorer 467	3
54	The Sneug	Foula	8/5	Explorer 467	3
55	The Noup	Foula	8.8/5.5	Explorer 467	3–4
56	Ward of Bressay and the Ord	Bressay	15/9.4	Explorer 466	5–6
57	The Noss Head Nature Reserve	Noss	10/6.3	Explorer 466	3–4
58	Virda Field and Mauns Hill	Papa Stour	11.5/7.2	Explorer 467	4–5
59	Ward of Clett	Whalsay	3.9/2.4	Explorer 468	2
60	Housay and Mio Ness	Out Skerries	8/5	Explorer 468	3–4
61	Lunna Ness	North Mainland Shetland	18/11.2	Explorer 468	5–6
62	Ness of Hillswick	North Mainland Shetland	7.2/4.5	Explorer 469	2–3
63	Esha Ness from Tangwick	North Mainland Shetland	14.5/9	Explorer 469	5–6
64	Ronas Hill	North Mainland Shetland	15.5/9.6	Explorer 469	5–6
65	The Beorgs of Skelberry	North Mainland Shetland	6.4/4	Explorer 469	3–4
66	Point of Fethaland	North Mainland Shetland	11/6.8	Explorer 469	3–4
67	South Ham	Muckle Roe	10.6/6.5	Explorer 469	5
68	Old Haa and Heoga Ness	Yell	4.2/2.6	Explorer 470	1–2
69	Ward of Otterswick	Yell	12.9/8	Explorer 470	6–7
70	White Wife	Yell	6.5/4	Explorer 470	2–3
71	Stuis of Graveland	Yell	11.7/7.3	Explorer 470	3–4
72	Gloup and North Neaps	Yell	13.5/8.4	Explorer 470	2–3
73	Valla Field	Unst	8/5	Explorer 470	2–3
74	Keen of Hamar	Unst	1.9/1.2	Explorer 470	1–2

Walk		Island	Distance (km/miles)	Map	Time (hours)
75	The Horns of Hagmark	Unst	8.4/5.2	Explorer 470	3–4
76	Wick of Skaw	Unst	1.6/1	Explorer 470	1
77	Hermaness National Nature Reserve	Unst	9/5.6	Explorer 470	3–4
78	Lamb Hoga	Fetlar	4.8/3	Explorer 470	1–2
79	Funzie Ness	Fetlar	5.9/3.7	Explorer 470	2–3
80	Vord Hill	Fetlar	7.2/4.5	Explorer 470	3–4

The Ring of Brodgar at sunset

NOTES

NOTES

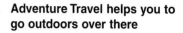

LISTING OF CICERONE GUIDES

For full and up-to-date information on
our ever-expanding list of guides,
please visit our website:
www.cicerone.co.uk.

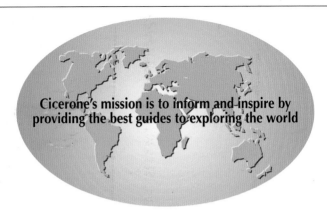

Cicerone's mission is to inform and inspire by providing the best guides to exploring the world

Since its foundation over 30 years ago, Cicerone has specialised in publishing guidebooks and has built a reputation for quality and reliability. It now publishes nearly 300 guides to the major destinations for outdoor enthusiasts, including Europe, UK and the rest of the world.

Written by leading and committed specialists, Cicerone guides are recognised as the most authoritative. They are full of information, maps and illustrations so that the user can plan and complete a successful and safe trip or expedition – be it a long face climb, a walk over Lakeland fells, an alpine traverse, a Himalayan trek or a ramble in the countryside.

With a thorough introduction to assist planning, clear diagrams, maps and colour photographs to illustrate the terrain and route, and accurate and detailed text, Cicerone guides are designed for ease of use and access to the information.

If the facts on the ground change, or there is any aspect of a guide that you think we can improve, we are always delighted to hear from you.

Cicerone Press
2 Police Square Milnthorpe Cumbria LA7 7PY
Tel: 015395 62069 Fax: 015395 63417
info@cicerone.co.uk www.cicerone.co.uk